eal Stories About God Showing Up in the Lives of Teens

TRUE

vol.1

Real Stories About God Showing Up in the Lives of Teens

TRUE
vol. 1

irene dunlap

True Vol. 1 - Real Stories About God Showing Up in the Lives of Teens
Copyright © 2003 by Youth Specialties

Youth Specialties Books, 300 South Pierce Street, El Cajon, CA 92020, are published by
Zondervan, 5300 Patterson Aveune SE, Grand Rapids, MI 49530

Library of Congress Cataloging-in-Publication Data

TRUE : real stories about God showing up lives of teens / general editor,
Irene Dunlap.
    p. cm.
Summary: A collection of real-life stories of God's presence in personal
situations, both the ordinary and the more challenging, that help reveal
the true nature of God in the universe and His work in people's lives.
  ISBN 0-310-25268-7 (v. 1 : pbk.)
  1. Teenagers--Religious life. [1. Christian life. 2. God.] I. Dunlap,
Irene, 1958-
II. Title.
  BV4531.3.T78 2004
  242'.63--dc22
                                                              2003015784

Unless otherwise indicated, all Scripture quotations are taken from the Holy Bible: New
International Version (North American Edition). Copyright © 1973, 1978, 1984 by
International Bible Society. Used by permission of Zondervan.

Web site addresses listed in this book were current at the time of publication. Please
contact Youth Specialties via e-mail (YS@YouthSpecialties.com) to report URLs that are
no longer operational and replacement URLs if available.

Editorial and art direction by Rick Marschall
Editing by Janie Wilkerson
Proofreading by Linnea Lagerquist
Cover and interior design by electricurrent
Design assistance by Sarah Jongsma
Printed in the United States of America

05 06 07 08 09 / DCI / 10 9 8 7 6

We know also that the Son of God has come and has given us understanding, so that we may know him who is true.
—1 John 5:20

Table of Contents

3. He is a God of Mighty Power   105

4. He is a God of Mercy and Forgiveness   159

5. He is a God of Wisdom and Patience   195

Dedication

This book is dedicated to teens and young adults everywhere who are seeking to know the truth about God and to those who know it and are willing to share it with others. I also dedicate it to Marleigh, whose faith and walk have been a huge inspiration to me, and to Weston, whose heart God has surely captured.

Acknowledgments

Above all, I thank God for his faithfulness, perfect timing, direction, mercy, and grace at every turn during the development of this project. May it honor and glorify his works and name beyond my highest prayers, desires, thoughts or hopes.

Thanks to four very special people who brought enormous heart to this project: to Patty Hansen for taking it as far as you could with me and for being the friend and partner whom I can truly admire and continue to make an impact with; to Juan Casas for your creative gifts, connections, and for being in the middle of it all, on the sidelines or wherever you were needed but always with belief in this project and in me; to Gina Romanello for absolute faithfulness in every aspect of development—I could not have kept on schedule without you, your incredible skills and willingness to do whatever it took to bring this one in—you truly rock; and to Brittany Shaw for helping locate the files when they tried to hide from me, and for your dedication to searching out stories. I love and thank God for each of you.

Thanks to my husband Kent and my kids, Marleigh and Weston; to my mother, Angela Jack and my in-laws Hank and Bonnie Dunlap; to my sisters, Kathi Fischer, Pattie Buford, Pamela Brown, Jeffra Lokteff, Greta

Dunlap and Lisa Vitello, and their families; and to my friends Jane Helmeczi, Ellen Fowler, Deborah Calvert, Laine Latimer, Marcia Kirschbaum, Deirdre Moore, Jennifer and Eric Briner, Stacey and Rocky Robbins, Tami Walsh, Christine Vile, Jill Shannon, Cherie Price-Steiner, and Danette Brugger for your constant love, encouragement, and support.

To those on our readers' panel, most of whom read over 100 stories considered for this book, thank you for your dedication and willingness to help us choose stories that will enable teens and young adults to see the heart of Christ: Brandon Aleson, Jennifer Birney, Arik Brown, Lauren Celek, Courtney Cheney, Tamera Collins, Marleigh Dunlap, Robert Kuhn, Josh Kaminsky, Taylor Lobdell, Nicole Marris, Jessica Schwarzberg, Chelsea Whitfield, and Amanda Woods. A very special thanks to the "Core Four," Arik, Brandon, Lauren, and Marleigh, for going the extra mile and for your commitment to the process.

To the following organizations and people, thanks for supporting this project, helping with story leads, getting youth to share their opinions, and for your overall encouragement: Erik and Leslie Williams, The Crossing; Jerry Huson, Biola University; John Davis and Londi Howard, DCLA; Lane Palmer and Debbie Bresina, Dare2Share; Brad Bennett, Real Ministry; Boogie Rose, Debbie Smith, Josh Beauchaine, Jeremy Armstrong, and Ken Clark, Young Life; Brett and Lynette Janzen, Newport Mesa Christian Center; Todd King, Coast Hills Community Church; Jon Irving, Yorba Linda Friends

Church; Eric Wakeling, Calvary Church Santa Ana; Chris Camden, Harvest Crusade; Greg Austring at Vanguard University; Ryan Skagerburg, Lighthouse Church; Becka Wegener; youth pastor Tim Hogan; Jon Greene, Saddleback Valley Christian Schools; and Mary Perdue, Youth Builders, for a lifelong friendship and for your advice and encouragement.

Thanks to Dave Bean for creating and turning around in record time a great Web site design, to David DeJonge for gifting me with your extraordinary talent and a much overdue new photo for my projects, and to Dee Dee Romanello for helping straighten out the books and for hanging in there through it all.

To the following people in artist relations, thanks for helping coordinate stories and supporting the development of the project:

Scott Brickell and Kim Nehs for Audio Adrenaline at Brickhouse Entertainment; Renee Hudson, who initiated T-Bone's story; Monica Fancher, Director of Marketing and Creative at FlickerRecords, and Desmarie Guyton, management for T- Bone; Lance Brown at One Moment Management for Joe Nixon and Slick Shoes; to Lori Lennon at Side 1 Dummy Records; to Seth Ebel, former P.R. Director at Tooth and Nail Records; Lisa Brinker at Mercy Ministries, for your efforts and resulting miraculous connection; Chris York of Sparrow Records, for all the contacts and tons of encouragement; and Leanne Bush, for your gracious assistance at the onset of the project.

Finally, to editor Janie Wilkerson, for your excellent work in refining the manuscript, and to Mark Oestreicher, Mike Atkinson and Rick Marschall at Youth Specialties, thanks for your faith and help in bringing this project into being.

Bless you all!

Introduction

If you're holding this book, reading these words, you likely have plans to continue on. If that's the case, I'm excited for you.

Without a doubt, the stories included in this collection have the power to help you better understand the God of the universe, no matter how well you know him now. The people who have shared their stories and lived these experiences have seen his unfailing love in everyday moments as well as the harder, tougher ones. The bottom line is always that his presence in their personal situations made it undeniably evident to them that God is indeed alive, well, and living among us, just as he always has been and always will be.

Misconceptions about God's true character often rob us of his incredible love. More than anything, I hope to point you toward a relationship with him and his son Jesus Christ by showing you how he works in our everyday lives in amazing ways. Our loving creator is protective, compassionate, wise, patient, powerful, faithful, and more. Although his word tells us about his wonderful ways over and over again, sometimes we need to see him at work for ourselves in order to truly understand him. That is what the writers in this book strive to do. It's kind of like this:

> One generation will commend your works to another; they will tell of your mighty acts. They will speak of the glorious splendor of your majesty... they will tell of the power of your awesome works... they will celebrate your abundant goodness and joyfully sing of your righteousness.
> **—Psalms 145:4-9**

Those verses go on to describe God this way:

> "The Lord is gracious and compassionate, slow to anger and rich in love. The Lord is good to all; he has compassion on all he has made...Your kingdom is an everlasting kingdom, and your dominion endures through all generations. The Lord is faithful to all his promises and loving toward all he has made. The Lord upholds all those who fall and lifts up all who are bowed down. The eyes of all look to you, and you give them their food at the proper time. You open your hand and satisfy the desires of every living thing. The Lord is righteous in all his ways and loving toward all he has made. The Lord is near to all who call on him, to all who call on him in truth. He fulfills the desires of those who fear him; he hears their cry and saves them."
> **—Psalms 145:13-19**

In sharing their stories with you, the contributing authors have also helped me fulfill my desire to obey one of God's directives in the Psalms—

> "Publish his glorious acts throughout the earth. Tell everyone about the amazing things he does. For the Lord is great beyond description, and greatly to be praised."
> **—Psalms 96:3, The Living Bible**

To the best of my ability, I have answered that call in these pages.

On behalf of all the contributing authors and myself, I offer you the following verse:

> We are therefore Christ's ambassadors, as though God were making his appeal through us. We implore you on Christ's behalf: Be reconciled to God.
> **—2 Corinthians 5:20**

May this book help you find his heart, hold it in yours, and never let it go.

Irene Dunlap

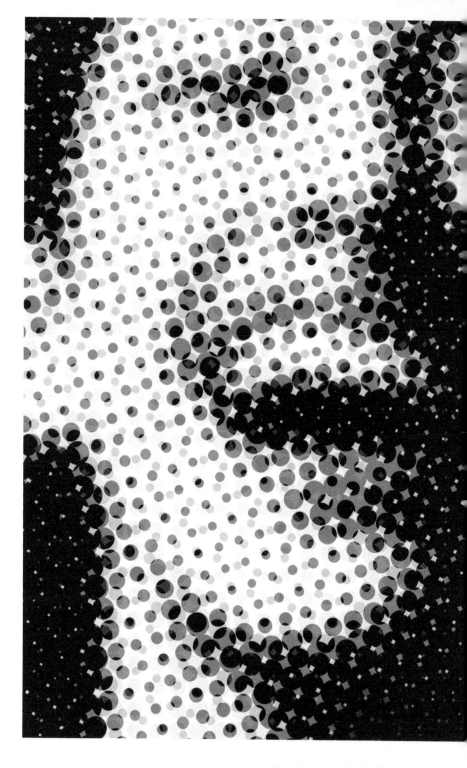

01

He is a God of
Protection

"The Lord will keep you from all harm—he
will watch over your life."
—**Psalm 121:7**

"You are my hiding place; you will protect
me from trouble..."
—**Psalm 32:7**

"I am with you and will watch over you wherever you go, and
I will bring you back to this land. I will not leave you until I
have done what I have promised you."
—**Genesis 28:15**

Under Control

"Because he loves me," says the Lord, "I will rescue him; I will protect him, for he acknowledges my name."
—Psalms 91:14

We sat there on the curb, watching photos of my family drift eerily, slowly into the street, their edges glowing and gradually turning each photo into black ash. One family memory after another—gone.

It was the fourth of July. Actually it was the fifth, very early in the morning. We weren't touring then, so we had hung out all day having a barbecue with friends. Afterward, we went back to my house; my parents were gone on a business trip about an hour away. We decided to watch one of our favorite movies of all time, *Rad*. It's like the greatest movie in the whole world.

Pretty soon a friend named Gary showed up and we stayed up until at least three, eating popcorn and watching more movies. Finally, only Dave, Gary, and I were left. Since it got so late, we all crashed in the bedrooms upstairs.

Only Dave heard the persistent pounding that woke him up about an hour later. It was pitch black. Someone was pounding on the front door and wasn't showing any signs of stopping.

Dave made his way into the hallway upstairs. Sparks were falling down through the entrance to the attic and into the hall on the second floor. The house was burning!

Dave ran back to where Gary was sleeping. By now, the noise from the fire was deafening. It sounded like a freight train was coming through. He woke Gary up and yelled at him to wake me and then get out. Then he ran back down the hall through the sparks and downstairs to see who was at the door. It was jammed. Whoever was on the other side had pounded so hard that it had messed up the door. Dave yanked and pulled until he finally got it open.

There on the front porch stood a guy that seemed pretty wasted. "Your house is on fire, man! You gotta get out now!" he screamed. His girlfriend was in the car in the driveway. He told Dave that she was calling 911.

Gary tried to wake me, but that's never an easy deal. I'm a very deep sleeper—pretty much nothing can wake me up. I just shouted at Gary to get away and turned over. Gary shook and yelled at me until I finally understood that there was a fire in the house. Finally, we made our way through the cinders and sparks, down the stairs, and into the front yard. We all stood in the driveway in our underwear, watching as the attic went up in flames.

Just then, a huge beam fell into my room, landing on my bed. The bed burst into flames. Seconds later, the whole attic crashed down into the rooms where we'd been sleeping. It happened that fast. If we hadn't gotten out right then, I wouldn't be telling this story.

Ash, burning cinders, and heavy smoke pushed us to the other side of the street. We sat down on the curb and stared at the burning house in disbelief. All of my equipment was now toast. Everything in my room was gone. Everything I owned was gone—except the boxers I was wearing. I ended up borrowing some clothes for us from my friend down the street.

Definitely the saddest thing was the sight of the photos from my parents' wedding falling into the street like little glow-in-the-dark squares.

We tried not to dwell on the stuff that had burned. We were just amazed and glad to have escaped with our lives. We had literally gotten out within seconds of the attic collapsing.

As it all sunk in, we started focusing on what God had done. All of the "what ifs" came into play. What if I hadn't invited friends over? I might not have gotten out if I'd been alone, since I sleep like a log.

The guy who woke Dave had been at a Fourth of July party and had gotten too wasted to drive himself home, so he had called his girlfriend to come pick him up. He lived a block from my parents. He and his girlfriend had been together for a few years and she had driven to his house hundreds of times before. That night, she made a wrong turn and happened by my burning house. How crazy was that? She knew the way to her boyfriend's house like the back of her hand. What if she had never made that "mistake?"

Later, we came to find out just how much protection God had sent our way.

That night, my older sister had awakened around three a.m. with a strong, nagging feeling of unease. As she tossed and turned, frustrated that she couldn't sleep, it slowly became clear to her that God was urging her to pray. She finally got up and went into the bathroom so that she wouldn't wake her husband. She later told us that she sensed that she was supposed to pray for my safety. She prayed steadily for an hour. Around four a.m.—the time that we got out of the house—she finally felt peaceful enough to go back to bed.

God had worked through someone who knew him well and then through someone who didn't seem to know him at all. He had it covered.

The firefighters determined that a bottle rocket had landed on the shake roof of the house. The fire had begun raging about the time that we fell asleep. Once the fire was completely out, they let us back in to check things out. My room was totaled. Then we went to the room Dave had slept in. The whole ceiling was gone. The only things that survived the fire were Dave's—his shirt, his pants and his Bible. They'd been protected somehow under a pile of stuff.

We never did go back to sleep, with all the fire trucks and the whole ordeal. We finally left to grab some breakfast and then went on to church. We were all pretty grungy and totally smelled like a campfire. The smell of smoke gave us a weird feeling for a long time after that.

Later that day, we went over to Dave's and sat around talking and writing about how, because of our relationship with God, we don't need to worry about things or danger or anything, really. He gives us everything we need to live.

In him, our lives are totally under control and we're free to just be.

> *...And if you think your life is under control*
> *And if you think you're living under control*
> *Cuz only the fool leaneth on his own*
> *And so I sing to You with all my soul*
> *Free to be without worry no more worry*
> *Yes I'm free, free to be without worry*
> *No more worry*
> *1 2 3 a.m. and the house is burning down*
> *4 a.m. the I AM grain of sand I am*
> *You woke me not to worry*
> *Yeah you woke me up not to worry*
> *But what should I drink*
> *What should I wear*
> *What should I eat*
> *Where should I sleep*
> *Who gives me everything*
> *So burn house burn house burn down*

Josh Auer
PAX217

Set Apart

...God is faithful; he will not let you be tempted beyond what you can bear. But when you are tempted, he will also provide a way out so that you can stand up under it.
—**Corinthians 10:13**

I've always felt that I didn't fit in. I was never the prettiest, never the funniest, and no matter how hard I tried, I always fell short to somebody in just about everything. This plagued me. Sure, I had friends, and I had a family who would give the Waltons a run for their money—but still, I didn't ever really "fit in."

When I was in seventh grade, we moved to a new town. Again, no matter what I did, I just couldn't fit in. Eventually, I found a few good friends, but I still longed for and struggled to be part of a group. This became blatantly obvious to me one night.

My freshman year, four of my closest friends were seniors. None of them were bad kids. They were actually pretty good friends to me. I even thought for a while that I fit in with them.

One night after a basketball game, I went into town with them. As we were driving along, one announced that we were going to go to his older brother's house to drink. Immediately a strong, heavy feeling of conviction came over me. I knew beyond a shadow of a doubt that I was not supposed to go there that night. My feeling of conviction was at war with my desire to fit in.

I struggled to find a way out, but it was about 10:30 p.m. and I was already in the car, on the way there. Let me not forget to mention how scared I was that these friends of mine wouldn't accept me if I turned them down.

"Let's go eat first. I'm hungry," one of them suggested. Whew, momentary relief. I decided that would give me time to think of a way to get myself out of the situation.

We got to a restaurant and I asked a girl with us to go to the restroom with me. When we got there, I told her that I didn't want to drink. She sort of laughed and said she wouldn't drink that night either, just for me. It made me feel a little better, but I still wasn't satisfied.

I remembered that my parents always told me that if I were ever in a situation that I knew I shouldn't be in, I could call them anytime, and they would come get me. I wanted to, but the fear of what everyone else would think scared me out of doing it.

Then it hit me. God said that he would always provide a way out. He was my only hope. I cried out to him, "Lord, I don't know how you're going to pull it off, but you said you would provide a way out of all bad circumstances. Please, show me a way out."

I went back to the table, hoping that my prayers would be answered. Because I was so nervous that night, I didn't eat. Minutes passed and my friends' food hadn't come. As a matter of fact, it took about an hour to be served in a restaurant that was usually fairly quick. By the time they got their food and ate it, it was nearly midnight, my curfew, and I had to get home.

Of course they were aggravated to have to change their plans because of me. After taking me home, they didn't want to have to drive back to town, so they went home, too. I know without a doubt that God showed me that his promises are real, and that he really does love us and take care of us.

My four friends were still my friends after that night, up until the day they graduated and moved on in life. Yet that was the last night that I ever tried to be like them in order to please them. In the long run, I think they saw my choices and respected them.

I've always known that I didn't fit in; I haven't always known that I've been set apart. Years of looking to God for guidance has shown me that I am set apart and was created for a reason. Rather than seeking acceptance, I now trust that God likes me just the way he made me. That has taken the pressure off so that I can concentrate on living the life that God has planned for me.

That's all that matters.

Meredith Breitling, 16

Really Real

Even youths grow tired and weary, and young men stumble and fall; but those who hope in the Lord will renew their strength. They will soar on wings like eagles; they will run and not grow weary, they will walk and not be faint.
—**Isaiah 40:30-31**

He said they were "free."

Hmmm…free…I didn't think so. The drug dealer handed two to my friend, Sandy. Then he placed two little pills in my hand. I stared at them, and a sentence that went something like this went through my mind: These pills will cost you your life.

I said, "No, thanks," and handed them back to him. Sandy said, "I'll take them."

Sandy became addicted. I became "marked."

Home life was tense with Mom and Dad going

through their own hard time. I didn't know how to process all of the emotional ups and downs, so between exploring and escaping, I turned to drinking and smoking.

The drug dealer was apparently impressed by the fact that I didn't take the pills. Oh, and he probably also noticed that I had come out of my "ugly duckling" stage and was starting to develop into an attractive young woman. I became his challenge.

Guys began calling me on the dealer's behalf: "He wants to see you." I was afraid of him, and yet I was intrigued, interested, and fascinated. Now someone was paying attention to me. That meant a lot.

So I kinda played this "come close, go away, come close, go away," game with the drug dealer. He was not happy. He didn't like games where he wasn't in charge of the rules. He wanted to win.

Halloween came and I went trick or treating. I was a black cat that year, I remember. I was 12 going on 18. The dealer hitchhiked across town, waited in a field by my house, and watched until I came home and went to bed.

And then he climbed into my room and raped me.

He threatened me, saying that if I told anybody or tried to yell for help, he would hurt my little sisters, and he would make it look like I was a whore. I didn't scream or cry out. My sisters were the most important people in the world to me, and I didn't want to risk their lives. And my reputation was so important to my family that I didn't want them to hear someone telling them that I was a whore.

The dealer began following me around, and he raped me over and over again for the next nine months. No place was safe. I was living in hell.

He told me that he wanted to give me a baby for my 13th birthday. So he raped me behind the church before my birthday.

I stopped getting my period. I thought I was pregnant. And I couldn't tell anybody.

I felt like I was dying inside. I can't describe how "nothing" feels, but I felt nothing, and hopeless, and forgotten. Definitely, totally betrayed.

Was this going to happen to me my whole life? Where was this God that I heard about every Sunday in church? Where was this Jesus? Either he didn't love me, or he didn't exist.

I convinced myself that he didn't love me. And if he didn't love me before this happened, why would he love me now—now that I've done all these bad things and had all these bad things done to me?

As it turned out, I wasn't pregnant. But from then on I walked around like an anorexic zombie—drinking, smoking, messing around with guys. I figured that I was already "ruined," so why not?

The one place I kept going was our church youth group. We sat in circles, and people talked about how much God loved us. I sat there, disbelieving, with my arms crossed on the inside and on the outside.

I'd ask questions like, "If God loves us, why are people dying?" "If God loves us, why are children starving?" "If God loves us, why are there natural disasters?"

The real questions I wanted to ask were,

Why am I dying inside?

Why am I starving inside?

Why does my life feel like a natural disaster?

The leader of the group took me out one day. We sat at a diner and ate bagels and drank coffee. After four hours of her being with me and telling me how much God loves me and wants to be close to me, I finally said, "You don't understand. He wouldn't want me."

She had such a knowing look in her eyes. "Stacey," she whispered, "no matter what you've done or what's been done to you, God can make you clean."

Clean? I thought. *I haven't felt clean in a long time.*

She drove me home and asked me if I was going to say yes to God being in charge of my life. I said, "Maybe...when I'm ready."

She turned and looked at me.

"I want to tell you two things: The Bible says that 'today is the day of salvation.' That means that if you've heard about God's love today, then today is when you respond. And the second thing is that the devil will always make you think you're not ready."

I said, "Okay..." She was a little too intense for my liking.

But when I walked into my house and headed for the bathroom, I stopped thinking about how intense she seemed, and I started thinking about how intense my situation was.

The bathroom is where I often went to get away from the world when things started spinning out of control. I took some pills and a razor blade from the medicine cabinet. I said, *God, I don't know if you're real, but I know that I can't live this way anymore. If the next 12 years are going to be like the last 12, then I'm not sticking around. So if you're real, I need to know right now.*

The room got all hazy and I felt like I was standing in the middle of a cloud—kind of like a huge blanket was hugging me. My insides started getting strong, the shame started disappearing, my hunched-over body began to straighten up, and my shoulders squared off.

God was there. It was undeniable.

"You're real, you're really real!" I said to the God I knew was listening. The God who was cleaning me up. The God who was loving me. The God who was changing me.

The God who was real!

I went to bed that night with such peace. I had not felt peace like this ever before. I had only felt numb.

I woke up the next morning, and that peace was still with me. I'd love to say that my whole world was different—that my family life was perfect and the guy who had pursued me had stopped stalking me... but that's not what happened. My situation didn't change. But I had changed!

My friends from youth group bought me a Bible. I read it day and night. Its words were such a source of comfort and hope for me. I even slept with my Bible at night, held it close, and to be honest, I even kissed it. There's still pink frosty lipstick on it. I loved God's word and how it spoke to me about forgiving others and myself and loving others and myself.

Forgiveness was a big deal. The drug dealer had done

some terrible things to me. Do you know what I told God? "You forgave me of everything I've done, so I forgive him for doing what he did to me." Incredible. Not only did I forgive him, but I started praying that he would know God and his love. I also prayed that God would give me strength to resist him.

One day, I was walking through the park by my house. The drug dealer was sitting on a big boulder, laughing at me and telling me to come to him or he would come after me. This strength rose up inside of me, and I yelled to him, "I am not coming near you. Not now, not ever again. You are going to leave me alone. God is watching out for me and you cannot bother me."

He left me alone. I'm not kidding. From that day on, it was done. Shortly after that, we moved, and I've never seen him again.

Other things began to change. Eventually I noticed that my language wasn't splattered with four-letter words. And I was so full of God's word and hungry for him that I didn't spend my time drinking and trying to run away from real life. Real life was becoming so exciting that I wanted to be fully alert for it.

And for the things that didn't change, like my home life, I found that I had new strength. I found that I could pray more for my parents and my sisters, for my friends and relatives. Over time, they all eventually said "yes" to God.

I learned the power of prayer.

I also learned that during the times when all that bad

stuff was happening, God was there, even when I didn't know he was. God used the bad stuff to help me see my need for him.

We live in a world that doesn't live in love. But that's not God's fault. I know God hears my prayers and cares about my needs.

What I know is that God is real.

Stacey A. Robbins

Miracle on Mother's Day

Whether you turn to the right or to the left, your ears will hear a voice behind you, saying, 'This is the way; walk in it."
—**Isaiah 30:21**

It was a call from a good friend that brought me all the way out to Nashville from Southern California. He and some of my other friends were about to be signed by a Christian record label, and they wanted me to be the drummer on the project. As usual, I prayed about the offer, looking to God for an answer. I wanted to go out there only if I could really grow and be effective for Christ in some way.

At last, I felt that God was telling me that I should give it a try. I had just gotten settled there about the time the contract was ready to be signed. Excited, we all went to the signing meeting. Something was telling me that I needed to really be thorough in looking at the offer. After a few hours of discussing it and really examining the deal, I still felt uncomfortable with signing it. I decided to pray about it over several days, often questioning myself as to why I would move out there and not end up joining the band. I would pray, "Lord, what am I doing?" But in the end, I had to trust that God was answering me when I ended up turning down the deal.

So, there I was, sitting around in Nashville, with my money dwindling and no record contract. I didn't know anyone there except one friend, Randy Williams, who was in a band called Big Tent Revival. We went out to lunch one day and I ended up telling him about my situation. I wasn't expecting or wanting him to do anything about it, but he offered me a position with the band on the spot—helping to sell merchandise at their shows. I responded with, "That's not what I came out here to do, but I would totally do that." I was just grateful for the work at that point.

I did random stuff that included selling t-shirts and posters and some other odd jobs. The following week, they needed to go to a big outreach gig in Oklahoma that was about five hours away. I expected to be selling t-shirts until Randy asked me if I'd consider driving the equipment truck for them. I was figuring a pick-up truck but when I asked, "Like, what kind of truck?" he said, "Well, it's one of those big Ryder-type trucks." I'd seen a lot of those on my way out to Nashville. Then he added, "It's a 24-footer." That seemed like a little more truck than I was prepared to drive, so I asked, "Don't you need a special license to drive one of those?" He said that it was the biggest truck you could drive with a regular class C license. I thought it sounded a little crazy but told him that I would do it.

We met to leave for the gig at about five in the morning on Mother's Day. When I saw the truck I thought, *Oh my gosh, this thing is huge!* But Randy assured me not to worry; that the driver of the tour bus would keep an eye out for me. So I shook it off with, "Alright—no big deal."

I climbed up into the truck and got behind the wheel, which was enormous. I'm 5'8", 130 pounds—not the biggest guy in the world—so it was kind of awkward. Still, I decided to be a good sport.

About an hour into the trip, I had just started to feel more comfortable with driving the truck when it began to get a little misty out. It was getting kind of foggy, too. There was a lot of dew on the windshield, so I turned the wipers on, but nothing happened. There were no wipers! It began to get harder and harder to see, and pretty soon, I began to lose sight of the taillights on the bus. I tried to keep up by doing about 65, but the bus just faded further into the distance. Obviously, the driver wasn't looking back to see if I was behind him. I got left in the dust... well, mist.

I began to mess with the knobs on the dashboard to see if I could get the wipers going when I hit a big bump. The truck jolted. Wondering what had happened, I rolled down the window to see what was going on. The truck was heading down an embankment toward a bunch of trees. I tried to correct the truck and get it back up on the road while screaming, "Lord—what do I do? Help me—this is crazy!"

The steering wheel was huge, but I wrestled with it while gently pumping the brakes and somehow got the truck back up on the highway. It was a miracle that the truck didn't roll at the speed I was doing, especially since the 18,000 pounds of concert equipment in the back had shifted to the right.

Just as I thought I was getting the truck under control, the front tire on the driver's side began to lift up. I started freaking out, trying to think about how to handle this one. Suddenly, the rear left tire lifted and I was rolling down the wet highway at a 45-degree angle doing a classic Dukes of Hazzard move on two wheels. The equipment in the back started crashing around—the roar of metal hitting metal was deafening.

I white-knuckled the steering wheel to keep from falling through the passenger side window onto the ground. At that point, I knew the battle was over. The truck slammed into the highway and the glass blew out of the passenger window. The horrendous screeching noise from the side panels of the truck sliding along the road made it nearly impossible to hear my own thoughts. As glass flew up into the cab, I thanked God that I wasn't down in the broken glass skidding along the highway.

After crossing all the lanes, the truck spun around and was now in the fast lane facing oncoming traffic.

I clutched the steering wheel, sort of hanging there in total shock. The driver's side door was facing the sky, heading straight up. I could hear the wheels still spinning and an eerie creaking and moaning from everything settling in back.

Then out of nowhere, I heard a voice—this full-on Oklahoma drawl—shouting, "Boy, you all right?" I thought I was dreaming. Then it came again—"Boy, you all right?"

Suddenly, this man who was like at least 70, was standing on top of the door. He had somehow popped himself up on the truck and now had the door open. "We gotta git you outta here—this thing's gonna blow!" he hollered.

"I've gotta get my stuff," I told him. "My bag is down there and it's got my stuff in it." I was totally freaking.

"No, you don't," he said, shaking his head. Then he grabbed me and just pulled me out of the truck. We jumped down and walked about 300 yards away in case the truck blew. The engine was hissing, and liquid was leaking out. Everything in back was so mangled that one of the lighting trusses was poking through the side of the truck.

I stood there in a daze. I wasn't wondering if my back or neck was messed up or anything like that. All I could think of was that I had to get the equipment out and to the gig somehow. The guys would freak if I didn't show up, and thousands of teens were going to be really bummed if the band wasn't able to play the gig that night.

Well, thankfully, the truck didn't blow up. The Highway Patrol showed up and then a huge semi tow truck came along to get the truck right side up. The equipment in the back just roared as it smashed around again. It was crazy. I was thinking, *Oh man, they're gonna kill me*. There was no doubt that the truck was totaled. There was also no way I was driving it away.

I asked the tow truck driver if there were any places around that rented trucks. He raised his eyebrows and with a look of disbelief he said, "Are you kiddin'? It's Sunday at 7:30 a.m., we're in the middle of Oklahoma, and it's Mother's Day. There's no way, man."

I wasn't about to take no for an answer. I decided that only God could make this happen, so I began to pray for a miracle. Finally, about 15 minutes later, the tow truck driver said that there might be one spot he knew of that could be open. He got on his radio and called, and sure enough, they were open and had one 20-foot truck available.

"Great, let's go," I said. He just looked at me like I was nuts. "I can't take you there. I have to get this truck to the junkyard, and then I have a ton of other calls to make." I pleaded with him to give me a ride. I gave him the whole story about the thousands of people that were expecting me to show up with the equipment. Finally, he agreed to take me with the crashed-up truck in tow.

The rental fee for the new truck was $1200. I absolutely did not have that kind of money in my account, but I gave the lady at the rental place my debit bankcard, held my breath, and prayed. She ran the card, and miraculously, everything went through. I was like, *God, this is nuts! You have to have been behind this one.*

That was the first hurdle.

Next, I had to find a way to get all the equipment into the new truck. The tow truck driver told me to follow him to the junkyard. Now, he was this super short guy, probably about 5'5", 180 pounds with a handlebar mustache and a huge cowboy hat; he totally looked like Yosemite Sam. There was physically no way that I could have moved all the equipment by myself. No way. I just looked at him, and without actually asking for his help, said slowly and deliberately, "I have got to get all of this equipment out of the old truck and into this one." I realized that he had already spent an hour and a half helping me, and I had heard tons of other calls come over his CB radio. I knew that he had a wife and a kid and that it was Mother's Day.

At the same time, I was super desperate.

I decided to just try to do it myself. I opened up the back of the crashed truck, and things were even worse than I had imagined. Everything was a tangled mess. Some stuff was totally broken. I started taking things apart when I heard something rattling behind me. I turned to see the tow truck driver lifting a big speaker off a broken light. I was so thankful, but I quickly thought to myself, *he's probably going to leave in 15 minutes. I'd better ask him to help me with the stuff that's too heavy for me to move.*

An hour and a half later, we were still just untangling things. It was the craziest physical labor I'd ever done. It took about three and a half hours to get the stuff into the new truck. The whole time, the CB had been going off constantly, but the driver stayed and finished the job with me. When we were finally done, I looked at him and said, "You have been such a blessing. I know you blew off all your other work to help me, and that was insanely cool. I can't pay you now, but can I get your address and send you a check when I get home?"

He shook his head and in a very nice way simply said, "Nope. Get outta here."

I thanked him in every way I knew how, hopped up into the truck, and started back down the highway.

It was then that I realized that I had to overcome one final hurdle: I had no idea where I was going! All the papers with directions to the gig had flown out the window in the wreck. All I knew was that the town was off Interstate 65 and that the gig was in a bowling alley. I had no idea how to get to Interstate 65. I got off the road and asked for directions at a gas station and found out that there were like three towns with the same name. We figured out which one it must be, and I headed out, still with no specific directions as to how to get to the gig.

I was totally at God's mercy and began to pray for him to guide me. I drove along I-65 for about two hours until I got to the town. I didn't know the exit or anything, so I asked God to tell me where to go.

Then the craziest part of the whole thing began to happen. I'd ask, "Here, Lord?" Do I go here?" I wouldn't hear him audibly, but I felt like he was answering me through this sense of peace and confidence at certain times. I'd get to a point where I'd need to go right or left, and I'd sense his answer.

I headed down a road off the freeway exit and drove for about ten miles. I felt like God was saying, "Keep going; keep going," so I did. Then, as I was rounding a bend, I spotted the tour bus. I swear it was an absolute miracle. It was crazy. Finally, the gnarliest day of my life was about to end. At this point, I was so exhausted, overwhelmed, and relieved that I noticed I was crying.

As I drove up the road, I could see the manager jumping and waving his hands in the air. He'd called the Highway Patrol a few hours earlier to see if they knew what had happened to me. When he realized I probably wasn't going to make it, he found a local company to rent him sound equipment, and the show went on.

As I told him the details, he assured me that the truck and equipment were all insured so I didn't need to worry about any of that. I'd thought I'd end up owing them thousands of dollars. I felt like a dork, but I was one relieved dork.

I'd also thought the guys in the band were going to lynch me. Instead, they brought me up on stage, told the audience what had happened, and then prayed for me in front of thousands of fans. It was amazing. Afterward, people came up and were so concerned with what had happened to me that they hardly bothered getting autographs from the band.

Still, I rode back to Nashville on the tour bus feeling like a total failure. The whole thing about my coming to Nashville seemed like a bad dream. I hadn't joined the band I came out to be in, I wasn't even drumming for a living, I'd crashed this truck—I began to question if Nashville had been God's will or my own.

I decided to use the money from the gig to buy gas to get back to California.

It took about three days for me to get my stuff together to leave. As I was packing up my drums, I stopped to answer the phone. On the other end was the manager of a band called Out of Eden. He was wondering what my summer was looking like. I answered that I was going back to California. He said that the band had some concert dates lined up and wondered if I'd like to drum for them. After deciding to at least rehearse with them and see if it felt right, I went ahead and took the gig.

We ended up opening for Jennifer Knapp. Then, while on tour, her manager asked if I'd be interested in taking over for their drummer. After getting to know Jennifer, I decided that she had an amazing heart for God. I knew I'd be spiritually challenged to grow and to be effective for Christ.

It was then that I realized my prayers about moving to Nashville were being answered. It wasn't in the timing or the way I'd imagined it would be, but it felt right.

Some prayers are answered immediately and without logical explanation. Some are answered in the long run—in God's timing.

I've learned to trust in both.

Aaron Redfield

The Bottom Line

But I have raised you up for this very purpose, that I might show you my power and that my name might be proclaimed in all the earth.
—**Exodus 9:16**

God has come through for me and literally spared my life several times since I've come to know him. I came from the streets, but God saved me in more ways than one. I've been attacked more by guns and violence as a Christian than I was when I was in the world doing things I shouldn't have been—like jumpin' people and doing crazy stuff.

I decided that if I had lived crazy for the devil, I was going to live more radical for God. He deserves that and so much more for what he's done for me.

First of all, I was left for dead about six years ago because I was going out witnessing the gospel and was reaching gang members and drug addicts. The drug dealers started getting upset because their business was declining, so they put out a hit on me. 15 gang members came to my house at three in the morning and beat me with pipes, weights, and bats, and then they pistol-whipped me. When my friends found me and got me to the hospital, they couldn't believe that I had survived the attack. God had saved me from that situation even after the gang members left me there to die.

But the next time God showed up in a crazy situation and defended my very life came not long after that. He spoke to me in one of the scariest situations I'd ever been in and literally saved me from being murdered.

I had gone down to Compton in Southern California from the San Francisco Bay Area where I live. One day I was wearing 49er gear, which is all red. Up in Northern California the talk on the street is always, "Hey, waz up, Blood? How you doin', Blood? What's goin' on, Blood?"

In Southern California, there's a gang called the Crips whose members always call each other Cuz. The Bloods are a rival gang to the Crips.

One day, my friend and I were hangin' out when all these Crips came up to us. We could tell they were kind of upset seeing me all in red. They said to me, "What's up, Cuz?" Not thinkin', I came back with, "What's up, Blood?" They just stared at us for about a minute, and then they turned around and left.

Not long afterward, they came back with five or six more of their homies with bandannas over their faces, bandit-style, ready to kill us. They walked up to my friend and stuck a nine to his head. Then they put a gun in my face and said, "Get on the ground. We're gonna kill you."

So the next thing I know we're layin' on the ground like they said when I heard God speaking to me. I distinctly heard a voice telling me to get up. And I said, "God—you want me to get up?" and he said, "Yeah, I want you to get up because I wanna show you that I'm all powerful." Then he said, "You're not a gang member anymore, so you shouldn't die like one."

At that point, God's power just hit me, and I stood up. The guy started yelling at me, "I said get on the ground...get on the ground." But I turned around, and I was fearless because God was all over me. At that moment, I could understand how all the martyrs in China and Japan, Indonesia and Korea could just stand up and be ready to be martyred for Christ. That's what we need to be—living martyrs, just like he was for us.

I turned around with all the guns and shotguns pointed at my face, and I said, "You know what? I'm not a gang member no more so I'm not going to die like one." I got on my knees and began to worship God. I said, "God, I thank you because You are the King of kings and Lord of lords, and I thank You because You've delivered me, and this day I will be with You in Paradise."

The Bible says that demons flee when they hear the name of Jesus. Every one of those gang members dropped their guns and took off running. That's the kind of power that God has. So if that doesn't let you know that there is a God, well, I'm sorry, but you crazy!

The thing is, man, you have to really be on fire and know that God is with you at all times. I knew that God was with me. His word tells us, "I am the head and not the tail. No weapon formed against me will prosper." So I stood up and exercised my faith in Christ, and those guys dropped their guns and took off running.

To me, that's an awesome testimonial of God really being alive and looking out for his children. Ever since then, that has made me more radical, and that's what it's all about to me—him being lifted up. I don't want people leaving my concerts saying, "What a great rapper, what a great singer, what a great concert." I want them leaving saying, "What a great God."

That's the bottom line.

T-Bone

I'm Here

"For I know the plans I have for you," declares the Lord, "plans to prosper you and not to harm you, plans to give you hope and a future."
—Jeremiah 29:11

I complain about all the pressure I go through as a teenager these days and almost forget how just a couple of years ago I was eager to experience it all. Back then I didn't know if I would make it as far as I have. I would often think to myself, *Well, it's a win/win situation. If I don't make it, I will probably go to heaven considering the fact that I'm still young and haven't committed any major sins, so I will see the Father earlier than I expected. And if I do make it, I'll get a chance to experience what it's like to be a teenager.*

As a ten-year-old, the closest I'd come to experiencing teenage years was viewing the daily routine of teenage girls in '80s movies like Sixteen Candles. I would watch them sneak out to go see their boyfriends, stress over a pimple the night before a high school dance, or throw huge parties while their parents were away. I wanted to feel what it was like to do all of those things. I even thought it would be cool to experience the late-night cramming I'd seen them do the night before a midterm. Plus, I wanted to learn how to drive. Anyway, I guess you could say that now I sometimes almost lose sight of the fact that I should be thankful that I've made it this far. But I am.

I remember vividly, it was a Tuesday in October when I first got sick. I had had pain in my lower abdomen for about two weeks, and that day I had a fever of 103.6∞, which wouldn't go down. By midnight, I had been in an emergency room, had blood tests and X-rays done, and was then transported to a children's hospital about 30 minutes from where I lived. I didn't know what was wrong with me, but I was exhausted, and all I cared about was getting some sleep. Little did I know that what was really going on would change my life forever.

All I remember immediately after that was that I was being showered with presents and get-well cards. I felt like I was the last one to know what was really going on with me then. My parents were told of the possibility of cancer, and then that diagnosis was confirmed.

A couple of my mom's friends from work were visiting me when the doctor came in and asked to speak to my parents in the conference room. I don't remember being all that worried. I had my presents to play with and company to talk to. They came back—I don't know how many minutes later—and my mother began to cry just looking at me. Her friend pulled the curtain to comfort her and to keep me from getting upset. My dad sat down and began to explain. I had AML, a type of leukemia. He said one out of some number of kids get it—that it was the type of cancer that mainly adults and teenagers get. He went on and on explaining the treatment that I would have to undergo: chemotherapy, a bone marrow transplant, and possibly radiation therapy. I was going to lose my hair and get sick a lot. I don't remember what I was thinking, but the things he said turned into a blur.

I guess my aunt was there too, because I began to cry as he was explaining that my hair would fall out. "Don't worry," she said. "I'll buy you lots of hats!"

The following weeks I spent in and out of the hospital. I underwent treatment, a lot of times without even knowing it. I kept myself busy painting in the playroom, playing and coloring with all my gifts, and praying. I'm not one who can tolerate the slightest bit of pain, so I did a lot of praying. I don't remember worrying that much about the outcome of it all. I thought about my win/win situation and entrusted myself totally to God to protect me.

During that time, my family was tested for bone marrow compatibility in preparation for a transplant. Miraculously, they found a match. My younger sister Nicole was to be my lifesaver.

The time soon came for me to enter the bone marrow transplant unit. I was shown the room where I was supposed to stay for more than a month, and I became scared. It was half the size of a regular hospital room and was very isolated. Even the nurses had to avoid going in and out of the room as much as possible. All visitors had to scrub really well and wear a hat, a mask, and a suit to prevent me from being exposed to germs. I was going to have my immune system suppressed so that my body wouldn't reject the new bone marrow. As a result, I had no protection against any diseases. At this point, it was truly up to God to protect me.

On a positive note, I made a friend at the hospital. One night, about a week or two before I was to enter the isolation unit, we both couldn't sleep. "It's okay, Samantha," my friend said when I told him what was eating me up. "I've been in there. It's not so bad if you can figure out how to have some fun. When I was there I took a 10cc syringe and squirted the nurses with water!"

I entered the isolation room feeling a bit better, but it got to be really lonely there. My brother Jonathan and my sister were exposed to sickness in school, so they couldn't come to visit. Actually, Nicole was too young to visit me in the hospital—even though she had been my donor. I was hardly ever home to see either of them, so I really missed them.

The highlight of my stay was when I got two special phone calls that I will never forget. One was from my sister Nicole. She was still a little sore from her operation, but she was doing fine. She and my brother were spending the week with my aunt and cousins in Manhattan. She was excited because they had spent the day at a hands-on science museum, Central Park, and Chinatown. My brother scolded her because he said she was making me feel worse that I couldn't have gone too, but I was glad that she thought of me—plus, they promised they'd take me there one day when I was better.

The other call was from some of my classmates. They asked my teacher if they could call during lunch. I only spoke to a few of them, and the call only lasted three or four minutes, but they made my day like no one will ever know.

During my isolation, my dad got the flu, so my mom was with me every day. I had to take an antihistamine to prevent any allergic reactions to the medicine and blood transfusions I was receiving. It made me sleepy and kept me from feeling too lonely.

To everyone's surprise, I was let out after only four weeks. Still, the next several months were difficult. Because I had been confined to my bed for four weeks, the muscles in my arms and legs had atrophied. I was weak, and to add to that, I was diagnosed with another medical problem: damage in my shoulders and hips from the medication I was taking. I was in a lot of pain, and I could hardly walk. It took much longer than usual to walk the simplest distances. The steps I took were shorter because of the damage, and it was hard for me to climb even a sidewalk step. I offered every bit of pain to Jesus. He tells us to give our burdens to him to carry for us, so I took him up on it.

In spite of all this hardship, I managed to get well enough to go back to school. I came back around the start of the third trimester of sixth grade, having missed the last two trimesters of fifth grade and the first two trimesters of sixth grade. Before returning, I had a tutor at home, and my teachers sent me my work, so I didn't miss that much.

After I came back to school, my classmates nick-named me "Speedy," but I wasn't offended. It was just a way for them to joke with me, and I liked that name. I was as slow as a turtle, an animal that I love, as I pushed a backpack around on a cart.

By my eighth grade year, I managed to ride the bus. I wouldn't have missed that for the world—ever since kindergarten, the oldest kids got to sit in the back. Nothing could stop me from doing that.

Things are looking good now. It's been exactly five years today since I had my bone marrow transplant, and I've been in remission ever since. I'm now considered medically cured. I've gone from weekly visits to the clinic for check-ups to monthly ones and then on to just four times a year. My immune system is almost back to normal, and I'm leading an almost normal life.

I was accepted to Our Lady of Mercy Academy, the school I am attending now, and even earned a scholarship. I can't do a lot of physical activities and contact sports because my hips and shoulders are damaged permanently, but I've improved a lot. I can climb stairs without holding on to the rail or someone for support. Before, my best friend would help me up and down the sidewalk. As I began doing more of those things on my own, I realized just how far I'd come.

I didn't spend my early teenage years living like the girls in the movies did, but I didn't miss them completely. No matter what each day brings, whether good or bad, I try to remember to thank God for seeing me through and to keep in mind that at least I'm here.

Samantha Cojuangco, 15

Sudden Death

...for he guards the course of the just and protects the way of his faithful ones.
—**Proverbs 2:8**

Who would have thought that some of my best friends—the ones I played spin the bottle with, stole pumpkins with, painted water towers with, and got drunk with—were the friends I met at my church youth group?

I know it sounds hypocritical, but just because you go to youth group doesn't mean you're a Christian. In our youth group there were kids at all stages of Christianity—some that were fully committed and carried their Bibles even at school (Bible nerds) and those who were forced to attend by their parents. Then there were kids like me, with one foot in the door of Christianity and one foot out—we were the ones who formed our "clique." We were the ones who got together after youth group and had all the fun... or so we thought.

One time at youth group, my friend Eric and I decided to skip out early. We drove around for a while and then ended up stopping at a community auction—it was just one of those spontaneous things to do on a hot summer evening. Anything seemed better than sitting in that muggy youth group room.

We bought tickets and had fun bidding on things we knew we didn't want—it was just fun raising the bid when we knew other bidders were willing to pay big bucks for an item.

Afterward, on the way home, I remember saying to Eric, "My parents will kill me when they find out I bought a piano for 20 bucks! I don't even have a way to get it home. It will never fit in my dad's truck. And even if I do get it home, there's no room for it in the house. Maybe I can keep it in the garage."

"You're crazy, girl," said Eric. "At least I ended up with something practical. My parents can't complain about an old suitcase—I'll be able to use it for college next year."

"Maybe," I said, "if you can get the dust off. That thing is really old."

We continued laughing as I drove along the open country road. Soon we approached the large hill near Eric's house.

As we ascended, a car came out of nowhere, roaring over the crest of the hill—on our side of the road—right in front of me. There was little time to react, and from that moment on, everything I remember took place in slow motion.

I felt my hands slowly yet deliberately turning the wheel to the left, swerving away from the oncoming car.

The right front end of each car danced slowly around the other, with no space in between. Then my hands turned the wheel to the right, swerving back into my lane. Everything happened slowly, as if time had nearly stopped. I felt that someone or something had helped me turn the wheel—I couldn't have reacted that quickly on my own. It was so intense. We were a breath away from a head-on collision, a breath away from death.

I was pretty shaken up as I pulled over to the side of the road. I was trembling badly, and I wasn't speaking coherently. Eric knew I wasn't able to continue driving, so he guided me into the passenger seat and drove the rest of the way home.

When we arrived at his house, Eric got his suitcase out of the trunk and carried it into the house. Feeling something rattle inside it, he opened it up—thinking maybe it was a smaller travel bag. Instead, it was an old board game. It was called Sudden Death.

Eric and I looked at the game and then at each other. We got chills as we realized how close we had come to our own sudden death. Then, right there in his kitchen, we held hands and prayed, thanking God for his protection and for giving us that wake-up call.

Death can be sudden; you never know what can happen. I believe it was God's hand on the wheel that night. He wanted Eric and me to have two feet in the door, not one. Now that we have rededicated our lives to God, I know that if anything were to happen to either of us, we would be able to meet God face-to-face.

Would you?

Wendy Dunham

Tire Tracks

The Lord protects the simplehearted; when I was in great need, he saved me.
—Psalms 116:6

I grew up in your average suburban neighborhood. Every day before school, my mother would drop me off at the neighbor's house across the street on her way to work. When it was time to catch the bus, I would walk a block down the hill to wait with the other kids. I would usually wave to Mrs. Adee, a neighbor lady who would always stand in her big bay window and watch us until we boarded the bus. There were about five or six of us who, while waiting for the bus, would pass the time by telling jokes, trading lunches, or wiping our noses on our sleeves.

But there was one thing we all did that we had in common: we would keep one eye peeled, looking out for "The Kid Who Never Went to School." None of us knew his name, his age, or where he lived. We only knew that he would ride his bike down the hill as fast as he could, trying to scare us by coming as close as possible to the nearest and most unwary kid he could find.

One fateful day, he chose me. Maybe I was preoccupied with the boogers in my nose, I don't know. For whatever reason, my luck ran out that day and he zeroed in on me.

But that day was different. That day, he lost control of his bike and ran right into me. The impact of the collision knocked me into the street where a very surprised bus driver was preparing to pick up her usual pack of kids. At that point, I must have blacked out.

I don't remember the bus driver screaming.
I don't remember the neighbor lady running out to the bus stop.

I don't remember the "runaway biker" crying about not wanting to hurt anybody.

I don't even remember the bus tire pinning my head to the ground. That's right——my head was stuck *under the bus.*

Now this wasn't one of those short buses or anything. This was a full-blown yellow cruiser that had a capacity of about 4,000 screaming kids—and it was parked on my cranium. It being the late '70s, my hairstyle was a mullet. This would explain why my hair was caught under the tire.

Well, to make a long story more interesting, the bus driver and Mrs. Adee pulled me out from under the bus all in one piece. Of course I was crying. Interestingly enough, though, I was crying that I just wanted to go to school. I know. It doesn't add up. But that's the truth.

So the shaking bus driver put me in the front seat of the bus, piled the other kids in, and ran us all to school.

Later that day, school officials talked with my mother and told her what had happened. She didn't believe them at first. Seriously, how could a kindergartner survive a bus accident like that? But then she checked my head for any injuries and found me in good health, except for one small detail: tire tracks.

That's right. I had tire tracks on my head: a sure sign that I had looked death in the eye and didn't blink.

My mother was aghast that her little boy had been traumatized in such a way. But it never had an adverse effect on me. God protected me in that situation and in many more that would follow. He has a purpose for my life, and nothing will keep that purpose from being fulfilled.

I never talked to the "runaway biker." I never even saw him again. And I don't have the tire tracks on my head anymore. But I do have a story about how God has his hand on my life. And that, unlike tire tracks, will never fade.

Jason Kennedy
Cadet

02

He is a God of
Faithfulness

"Know therefore that the Lord your God is God; he is the faithful
God, keeping his covenant of love to a thousand generations of
those who love him and keep his commands."
—**Deuteronomy 7:9**

"For the word of the Lord is right and true; he is
faithful in all he does."
—**Psalms 33:4**

"Your love, O Lord, reaches to the heavens, your
faithfulness to the skies."
—**Psalms 36:5**

Solid Rock

He alone is my rock and my salvation; he is my fortress, I will not be shaken.
—Psalms 62:6

"Oh, Jesus."

The two words escaped my lips before wrenching sobs overtook my body. I laid my arms on the chair in front of me and quickly buried my face to muffle the noise. The walls of the chapel at Lutheran Hospital echoed my cries, and a large cross and a few rows of chairs were my only companions. The clock had struck midnight hours ago, but my family refused to leave Mom's side while she fought for her life in Intensive Care.

I had been so strong for my family all day, but I couldn't hold back my emotions any longer.

I had nothing left. Everything I held dear to me had been shattered by life's wrecking ball, and my world was in ruins. All I could do was bleed from the pain. I didn't know how much more of life's hard knocks I could take.

My foundation first began to rattle around Christmas. Dad called a family meeting, and that only meant one thing: something was wrong, and we needed to discuss and work it out as a family. Characteristic of Dad's forthright personality, he didn't try to soften the truth.

"We have no more money. You and Christopher will have to find a way to pay for your education by yourselves next year, or you won't be able to return to college in the fall."

The news hit me like a blast of dynamite. Pay for my college education myself? I couldn't come up with that kind of money in such a short time! I already had a job at college, but all of that money was paying off my second semester. Even if I worked all summer, I could never come up with enough to pay for an entire year of school.

I felt my stomach tighten into a ball of tension. I knew we were having financial problems, but I had never guessed that things were this bad.

The possibility of taking a semester or a year off from school terrified me. College had been my dream since I was ten years old. I loved everything about my new life—the independence, my classes, the campus, and my friends. The thought of postponing my dream and moving home to work a full-time job brought tears to my eyes.

I was scared, but I wasn't going to let fear overrule my reason. I knew that if God wanted me to remain in school he would provide a way. My foundations were shaken, but my trust in God did not collapse. God would take care of me and place me where I needed to be.

The next whack of the wrecking ball hit me in January. I came home for a weekend to visit my great-grandmother who was dying, but a phone call late Friday night knocked me to my knees. My brother's best friend and college roommate, Jake, had been in a serious car accident. He died Saturday afternoon just before I arrived at the hospital with my parents. Jake's death was very hard for my family and me. We had been neighbors for years, and my brother and I grew up playing with Jake and his brother and sisters. His death just devastated us.

Two months later, I found myself at the hospital again. The day of Jake's funeral, Mom had started running a fever. A week later she caught a cold. As each week passed, her cold progressively worsened until in March she landed in the hospital with pneumonia. The doctors treated her, but she still did not improve. They ran some more tests and diagnosed her with congestive heart failure. The virus that she had been battling for a month had settled in her heart, and her heart was functioning on less than 15 percent capacity. The doctors said the only thing keeping her alive was her will to live. The wrecking ball hit its final mark, and my world completely shattered.

As I sat alone in the chapel at the hospital, words could not express my pain as the ashes settled around me. I couldn't imagine life without Mom, and the anguish of possibly losing her was more than I could bear. I had been through so much during the past few months. When was this destruction going to end?

But even as I lay hurting and bleeding before my Creator, I felt him wipe away my tears. He eased the terror I felt in my heart and replaced it with his peace. I didn't know what the future held, but I felt God's strength lift me out of my life's ruins. I desperately clung to Jesus and promised that I would trust him no matter what happened. Suddenly, I knew everything was going to be all right.

Mom was released from the hospital two weeks later, but she was now an invalid. I moved home from college in May only to find our circumstances even worse. Our already tight finances had completely diminished. We were only a few hundred dollars away from bankruptcy. As Dad and I sorted through bills that we couldn't pay, we told each other that God would provide. He had seen us through this far; he wouldn't abandon us now.

During the summer months, I experienced God's faithfulness in a whole new way. People brought us meals three or four times a week so we didn't have to buy groceries. Women from the church came to clean our house every week for free, and men came to mow our lawn. We managed to pay all of our bills, and by God's grace my brother and I won several scholarships and both of us were able to return to college in the fall with a full ride.

God had filled our lives with abundant blessings, but his greatest blessing came at the end of June. Mom felt led by the Holy Spirit to be anointed with oil, so one Sunday we gathered in our pastor's office and laid hands on her and prayed for her healing.

Since that day, her health has progressively improved. Before the anointing, she could only manage to take a shower before she became completely wiped out. Now she can walk around most of the day and just experience light fatigue. Though the doctors didn't think she would ever be able to function normally again, my mom is almost completely healed.

Tough times are never fun to go through, but they are powerful teaching tools. My faith in God has grown very strong. When life had stripped me of everything, God never left my side. He was all I had left, and even though everything else was crashing around me, he never moved. He gave me strength when I had none; he gave me peace in my darkest moments. When life knocked me down, Jesus Christ held me up. Jesus proved to me that life's wrecking ball would never be able to crack or crumble his faithfulness to me.

He is the Solid Rock.

April Lynn Stier

On the Other Side

Many are the plans in a man's heart, but it is the Lord's purpose that prevails.
—Proverbs 19:21

I was the epitome of a bright-eyed, optimistic, and naive junior higher. Daydreaming about my future was my favorite pastime, especcially during math class. There were so many things that I was unsure about back then. There were things that I optimistically hoped for and some really impractical ones that were just far too much fun to neglect thinking about.

Still, two things prevailed in my mind as fact: when I turned 16, I'd have a boyfriend, and if I continued to work hard in school, I'd leave my small town after graduation and go off to college. It seemed simple enough, and I couldn't see it happening any other way. After all, these two things held true for many people I'd observed on television, in my family, among friends. I didn't see myself any different.

I left many daydreams at that small run-down junior high. Unfortunately I brought these two assumed "facts" with me to high school as though they were my favorite holey pair of jeans: no matter how much of a decomposed tribute to the nineties they had become, I couldn't part with the comfort. But as high school went along, I came to realize that the comfort I felt in my expectations was exactly the thing I had to let go of in order to grow into the person God wanted me to become.

High school flew by faster than I ever imagined. I kept busy with sports, advanced classes, and a variety of community activities. Every Thursday, I went to youth group at my church, because it was fun hanging out with the people there.

But I especially loved spending time with my five best friends. We spent countless hours together until I came to know everything about them, and they about me. It was a sisterhood of six, and I felt blessed to have them in my life.

As far as the "having a boyfriend at 16" expectation went, it hadn't happened by the time I turned 17.

Around that time my best friend shared with me how she had been fighting depression. She revealed that she was tired of battling and thought that the depression was finally going to win. It was hard to understand how someone like her—smart, friendly, talented, beautiful, with a loving family and endless opportunities—could feel this way about herself. I remember praying hard as tears streamed down my face for God to deliver her.

The remainder of that year, she seemed to be doing better, but I had begun falling.

In hindsight, it was as if her honesty triggered something in me and thrust me into the pit of depression. I couldn't pinpoint what I was sad about. All I knew was that I would cry myself to sleep only to wake up exhausted. In the following months I was basically bored and becoming more and more unhappy with the fact that I didn't see any immediate results in my mundane life. By the end of my junior year, I stopped pursuing my interests in sports and social events.

Then one day I just snapped.

Yelling in my prayers, I screamed at God, asking him why I was constantly in this miserable state. I told him that I didn't want this life anymore. It was too hard to have this mindset, and I was too weak to handle it. In my fury I screamed, "Take my life. I give it to you. I don't want to be in control. Do whatever you want!"

I quickly learned that those are some of the most empowering words a person can speak.

My life totally changed after that night. I began to focus less on myself. Before I knew it, reaching out to other people had become second nature. The more I gave, the more I learned that life was about the value of relationships with others and bringing glory to God.

This new mentality made life fun again. I got back to being involved in clubs at school and playing sports just for the fun I had with other people, not to improve my time or gain a CIF title. I started to attend youth group with the intent to meet the underclassmen. I chose to sit at a table in anatomy not where my friends were, but where my lab partner (whom I didn't know at the time) would eventually be introduced to Christ over dissecting a cat together. The value in human life and simple pleasures for God became my ambition and joy.

Then the true test of my faith came, unexpectedly and fast.

My five friends and I all picked different colleges to attend—in different parts of the country. We talked it out and decided that we'd have different experiences to share, so we allowed that excitement to outweigh the sadness.

I wanted to attend one particular private school, so I filled out an application and sent it with high expectations. I wanted more than anything to be in a Christian environment, and I assumed that God would want me there, too.

I was accepted but soon found out that because of my family's income, I was ineligible for grants. Then it became a catch-22 because the tuition was too much for my family to sacrifice. We were caught in between. The reality was that I would have to stay home and attend a junior college. My expectation of going away to college had suddenly crashed and burned before my eyes.

I fell fast into my old mindset. Angry and jealous that I didn't get to leave like all my friends did, I was also mad that I had worked so hard in high school only to go to a junior college. I couldn't even tell someone where I was going without my eyes swelling up with tears.

I was disappointed in my situation and in the cards God had dealt to me. But as time passed, he began to show me the little box I had placed him in.

My first year of college was seemingly uneventful. My friends would call to tell me all their exciting news about the people they had met and what funny thing had happened in the dorm. I was amused by their stories and happy for them. At the same time, I was often shocked at some of their new experiences.

My usual weekend excitement was spending Friday night on the couch zoning out on another "Blockbuster Favorite." I was surprised that it didn't seem to bother me as much as I thought it would and began to realize how God's grace was covering me. Slowly, I began to see how he was showing me his divine will for my life.

Over time, I began to love my school. It was no mistake that I sat next to a Christian in all five of my classes. The more I got to know my professors, I realized how amazing they were. I was able to take classes like art, yoga, and guitar—courses that would not have been available at the school I had wanted to go to. I'd also have been paying a lot more money there.

On top of all of that, being home brought me closer to my family. I learned more about who they were than ever before and gained a new respect for them.

I also learned who my real friends were: those who made an effort to keep in touch, who returned my calls no matter how exciting their new lives were, and who made time to see me when they were in town. Although I lost some of them, I gained closer, deeper friendships with those I valued and who valued me.

When God closed the door to leaving my small town to "better myself," he opened new ones. I became the junior high leader at church. Nothing has given me more satisfaction than to see young teens grow and develop little by little into the people God is leading them to be. Every Thursday I leave there excited as I see what God is doing in their lives, and I am honored that he has allowed me to be involved in them.

The change in direction brought even more opportunities my way. I never would have imagined that I could travel around the world and complete a semester of study at the same time, but that's what I ended up doing. As I traveled, I gained a much stronger perspective about how God is everywhere. I experienced an amazing fellowship as I shared the love of Christ in different countries. I learned an incredible, irreplaceable amount about life and the value that God has placed on all people, all around the world.

I believe that I learned more during the time I spent traveling with Semester at Sea than I would have at any other university. I wouldn't have had the finances or the time to do it if I had gotten my way and attended the college that I had wanted for the first two years.

God had these experiences planned for me, even as I cried that things weren't going my way. I realize that he took me at face value when I told him, "Take my life...Do whatever you want." I can see how he was probably staring down at me saying, "You'll be amazed, just hold on and wait."

Looking back, I wouldn't ask God to repaint one stroke in the artwork of my life. All of the emotional and spiritual pain that I experienced as a result of underdeveloped dreams, lost friendships, and earthly disappointments was far outweighed by what I gained.

I have gained trust, respect, and admiration for our creator, a true passion for life, an adventurous and free spirit, humility, humbleness, and irreplaceable joy. I keep in mind, when things aren't going my way, that if I keep my eyes on him, they are going the better way.

As far as the boyfriend expectation goes, well, I'm 21 and still haven't had that experience. I am five years off the schedule I made myself when I was 13. The way I see it, God hasn't revealed that part of the painting yet. Knowing that he'll take care of that aspect of my life as well as he's taken care of the others, I'll patiently wait till I'm 55 if I must to be amazed at the prince he has prepared for me.

I live life with joyous anticipation as I keep my eyes on God's plan for my life. I know that with him in charge, I'll continue to be pleasantly surprised. The intermediate confusion and disappointment will be well worth what he has waiting for me on the other side of it all.

Haley Vile

It's Your Call

Do not conform any longer to the pattern of this world, but be transformed by the renewing of your mind. Then you will be able to test and approve what God's will is—his good, pleasing and perfect will.
—Romans 12:2

It had been my dream to play college basketball and to become an actor/movie star for as long as I could remember. But even after a successful high school basketball career no coach showed even a shred of interest in me, and I didn't really know how to jump-start an acting career while living on a farm in Wisconsin.

With no other game plan in sight, my mom suggested I check out Seattle Pacific University. From the moment I stepped on campus it just felt right. So the summer after high school graduation, I packed up and headed for Seattle. I planned to get a computer science degree "to fall back on" since I really intended to pursue acting once I graduated.

Still hoping to play basketball while in college, I'd sent a tape of some highlights from my high school career to the coaches at SPU, and two weeks later, I got a call from the assistant coach. I jumped at the offer to try out and was accepted to the SPU men's basketball team.

I thought life could not have been any better, until I learned about the five to one female to male ratio at SPU. Life became flat-out perfect.

In February, the team took a trip to sunny Hawaii. We were winning, and I got a great tan, but we missed the critical first week of the second quarter. I got so far behind in my classes that I was in danger of not graduating. I was completely lost.

By that point, not only was my academic future unclear, but I was also frustrated by my lack of ability on the basketball court. It had become evident that I was the guy who only played in no-pressure situations, like when there were only five seconds left in the game and we were winning by 47 points. It really started to eat at me, and my ego was hurting.

I was pretty depressed, and the gloomy Seattle weather didn't help my mood.

So I decided to go to chapel one rainy morning. Chapel was something that my school held twice a week, consisting of an hour of singing praise to the Lord and listening to a speaker. Being in the presence of God always comforted me, so I was banking on some relief.

The speaker turned out to be a lady who looked like she was about 150 years old and spoke so softly you could hardly hear her. She had come to Seattle Pacific as a student when it was just a nursing school, but felt that the Lord had called her to spend her life in India serving the poor—and that is exactly what she had done.

That is all I remember her saying because I was hearing another voice in my heart that was much louder than hers. The feeling that came over me told me that it was unmistakably God's voice. It was as if he had laid both of his hands on my shoulders and was talking directly to me. It seemed so out of the blue, yet totally clear at the same time; he was asking me to give my life to youth ministry.

In my logic, the whole idea seemed so random. I did not see how my dreams of being an actor could fit into that scenario, so I tried to shrug it off. I told God to be quiet so I could listen to the speaker. Imagine that: God wanted to talk, and I was too busy to listen. But God was not going to let it slide, so he stayed on me.

Pretty soon, in self-defense, I began talking back to this inner voice. I gave God my little list of reasons why I could not be a youth pastor. Number one, I had dreams of becoming an actor, and number two, I did not want to be poor (and we all know that pastors have to be poor!) On top of that, I did not want to have to tell non-Christian friends or family members what I was doing for a living. They might not understand and I'd be embarrassed. This was just not going to happen.

So for the rest of the morning, I walked around campus arguing with the Lord. I remember standing in the middle of campus in the pouring rain with people all around me, but nobody seemed to notice me. It was just the Lord and me, face to face. He gently worked on my heart, reminding me of the fact that I had already pledged my life to him. I began to feel that if I ignored him on this one, I would not only be going back on a promise but also missing out on something really important.

So there I stood, crying like a baby, soaking wet and broken. Still, I wasn't totally ready to give up on the things that I thought I wanted. So before I agreed to say yes, I reminded him about my dreams of getting into the entertainment industry and my desire to not end up living in poverty. Then I gave my life, my dreams, and my desires to God and said, "Lord, I am accepting your call; the rest is up to you."

At that moment, I could feel the weight lift off my shoulders. Knowing that the Lord was now fully in charge of my life left me with an extraordinary, sweet peace. I changed into some dry clothes, headed straight for the admissions office and changed my major to Youth Ministries.

The summer after graduation, I got a job at Nordstrom. I was thinking I'd make more there than in youth ministry, but God had other plans for me. I found myself working at the Boys' and Girls' Club instead.

After that, I could hardly keep up with all the calls I got to work with kids. For the next year and a half, God totally blessed me, and things were just going crazy. I was making more money than I had dreamed of, and I got to pick and choose from the work he laid before me. I wasn't living in poverty after all.

After awhile I got a little too confident and began to forget where my blessings were coming from. The second that I said, "Hey God, you want me to work here, but I want to work at this other place," everything changed. I decided to do things my own way, and soon my life began to feel like I was swimming through molasses. Even my health went down the tubes. Then a sin that I had struggled with earlier in my life crept back in, and I was now dealing with that as well. I was a mess.

It took me months to get back on my knees and admit to God that I had blown it. I finally began to get that when I honored him, he honored me. And he didn't intend to rob me of my dreams, as I would come to see more clearly.

I prayed for God's guidance to lead me to the next thing he had for me. I felt like it was time to move on, but I didn't know where to go or what I should do.

In the back of my mind, Hollywood was still calling me, but I wasn't as eager to call the shots. Still, I had to get something going, so I thought I could get a job as a youth pastor in L.A., and maybe something in the entertainment industry would work out while I was at it.

I packed up and began driving south. When I got to the border of Oregon and California, I distinctly felt like the Lord was telling me that he had a perfect road trip planned for me. So I drove to wherever I felt he was taking me, ministering to people along the way and letting him take care of the details.

One day I ended up in Venice Beach. It was there that I accidentally left my ATM card in a machine. Before I even realized what I had done, my account had been wiped out, and I was officially penniless. It was really weird, but I had no fear or anger—not even the desire to go off on God about all my money being gone. I was completely at his mercy.

"I'll do whatever you're asking me to do; please just make it clear to me," I said to him.

Being broke with no job, I ended up back home in Wisconsin. It didn't take long before I was bored out of my mind from being stuck out in the middle of nowhere.

While hanging out, I caught a news blip about a new TV show. 16 people were being chosen to go to a deserted island together. It looked interesting, so I looked up the Web site and found out that if I wanted a shot at it, I had two days to get a tape of myself to the producers. So I went out into the cornfields with a video camera on the back of my truck and did the audition in just one take. The whole thing came to me and was finished within 24 hours.

Then I got on with life and pretty much forgot about it.

A few weeks later, I came home to a message from a guy named Fred Survivor. I thought, *Who's that?* I reminded my dad, who had taken the message, that I had applied to a show called *Survivor*. "Could that be what you meant?" I questioned him. It turned out to be a producer named Fred from *Survivor* who told me that I needed to be at an interview in Minnesota in a few days.

During the interview, I just acted like myself and was very comfortable with the producers. They couldn't believe that I had done my audition in one take in a cornfield.

Several weeks later, while on a skiing trip, I walked into the lodge and saw a message on the board that said, "Dirk Been, call home—important." I thought maybe someone had died or something. I called home to hear that "Fred Survivor" had called. I'd made the next round.

Before long I was on a plane to L.A. to go through another round of interviews as well as six hours of psychological testing and the most invasive physical I had ever had in my life. For ten days, I was interviewed by psychologists, producers, and directors.

On the tenth day, they took the finalists to meet all the vice presidents of NBC. I was asked to share what I was about with all of them.

I started the interview with, "All right, I'm a virgin. Any questions?"

Their response to that was, "What's your *problem*? Do you need a date or some help or something? Why would you live your life like this?"

So I laid it all out for them, and in the process, I shared the gospel with them. Their response was, "Okay, so you're a Christian. When was the last time you read the Bible?"

I pulled it out of my backpack. "About 20 minutes ago," I said.

They were kind of blown away.

I knew that the TV show was on the line, but I had decided to keep it real for the Lord rather than sell out. In front of all these non-believers, I stuck my neck out for the Lord. It was amazing. I thought, *Even if I don't get on the show, I just spent an entire hour sharing God's word with a bunch of TV producers in L.A.*

During the final interview, I was told to choose three things that I would want to take on the island with me. The producers said that they would then pick one of them and let me know what it would be. I told them that I didn't need three things—the only thing I needed was my Bible. If I couldn't take that, I wasn't interested in going.

They agreed, and I was accepted as one of the 16 chosen out of literally thousands of applicants.

I thought I would just be witnessing to 16 people on the island, but the show turned out to be a huge hit, and I was able to witness to *millions* of people—kids and teens included.

God hooked me up with a situation that included his dream for me and the one that I originally had for myself. *Survivor* ultimately opened up doors to other things, like speaking to kids' groups around the country, doing other TV shows, and having the opportunity to learn and grow in the craft of acting.

I know without a doubt that God does not give us dreams just to tease us with them and then take them away. Instead, he wants full control in our lives so that he can make our dreams reality, a hundred times better than we could have imagined.

You want to discover the Lord's call on your life? I am not going to lie—it may be the toughest thing to do—but just stop and listen!

It's your call. But trust me, if you do, you'll not only survive this life—you'll live out your dreams.

Dirk Been

Who I Am Today

*They will tell of the power of your awesome works,
and I will proclaim your great deeds.*
—Psalms 145:6

Has your world ever been turned upside down? Mine
has.

Before my world changed, I was a normal 14-year old.
I had many friends—some my parents would be proud of,
others they would have preferred me not to hang out with.
The problem was that I cared about my friends, if you can
call that a problem.

When I discovered that some of my friends were
doing things they shouldn't do, I tried to get them to
change. I remember thinking that if I had something in
my life that others did not have, I could make a difference. So, one day I did something that I'm convinced
changed my life. I prayed. I asked God to give me a
"stronger testimony."

What was I thinking?

One day, I noticed a knot on my neck. I told my parents, but we didn't do anything right away. Soon it began to grow and to hurt. Finally I went to the doctor, and that's when my entire world was turned upside down.

The doctor told us that I had six tumors in my neck and chest, ranging from the size of a quarter to the size of a softball. All of a sudden, I was living with something that most people my age didn't even think about: cancer. Hodgkin's Lymphoma is a cancer that attacks the lymph nodes, and I had it.

I vividly remember my dad sitting next to me crying while he tried to explain it to me. Then the doctors described my treatment to me—18 rounds of chemotherapy, six weeks of radiation, and then a re-evaluation to determine the next step.

When I began my treatment, things got hard—really hard. I grew very weak and sick. I was an athlete, but just walking from my bedroom to the living room ten feet away became an exhausting chore. I couldn't do anything, couldn't go anywhere. My hair fell out, I gained weight, everything made me sick, I had constant headaches, I was always puking, and I felt like crap all the time. I was allergic to practically everything they gave me. Reactions to the chemo, rashes from the medicine, and constant fatigue were a daily part of life.

Every time I went to the hospital for treatment, what should have been a few hours in the clinic turned into days, because I'd end up being admitted. I hated doctors coming in all the time, poking around, and then leaving.

Radiation wasn't any better. It made me nauseated and I was always tired.

I was tired all right—tired of all this crap. I just wanted life to be like it was before, but things had really changed. I was diagnosed just one month before summer vacation, so while school was still going on my friends called all the time and were concerned about me. They did cool stuff like writing me letters and turning my locker into a shrine.

But when summer came, my friends disappeared. Maybe they just didn't know what to say any more or what to do. But one thing I do know is that they were *gone*.

I remember calling my friends one day, and all of them were either too busy to talk or gone having fun. My life sucked! I had to stay home all day by myself. I remember crying myself to sleep many nights because I just wanted it all to go away. I was tired of it all.

When my friends did call, all they asked about was how was I doing, and then after I repeated what the doctors had said for the hundredth time, they had to go. Needless to say, I found out who my real friends were. Out of all my friends, only a few stayed. They would call every now and then, but after a while I just got tired of talking to them because they always asked, "How are you doing?" "What do the doctors say?" I just wanted to scream, *I have cancer! How do you think I'm doing?* When I felt like talking, they were not around.

One night I was lying on the couch, staring at my eighth grade picture on the wall. I just stared and cried. My life had changed so much. I just wanted it all to go away. Life was hard. Hospital visits, radiation, chemotherapy, ambulance rides to the emergency room, bleeding uncontrollably from my nose, and gasping for breath. What a life! I was ready for it to all go away.

With no one else to turn to, I called my youth pastor, Josh, and shared with him how miserable I was and how none of my friends had any time for me anymore. He listened to me and then encouraged me to call them again and give them time to adjust.

I just cried. I was tired of the adjusting. Why weren't my friends here for me? I was the one with cancer.

A few days later, Josh showed up at my house to visit. He began coming over and hanging out with me on a regular basis. He would bring work over and do it sitting on my living room floor, or he would bring me some things that I could do for him. He kept me busy, and it helped the days to go by much faster.

I soon learned that I could go to Josh with anything. I could cry, yell, cuss, get mad—and he would just listen and let me get it all out. He helped pull me through some of the hardest times just by being there and listening to me.

Now I'm 16, and I'm in remission. I still have to wait until I'm 19 to use the word "cured" but life is a little easier today. I still get tired a lot and can't do all the things I used to do. The chemo and radiation have caused side effects that I'll have to live with for the rest of my life. But my life is getting back to normal, sort of.

Life before I had cancer is now a faint memory. My life has been changed forever. Looking back, I realize that from the time I was diagnosed with cancer, I have never been afraid. Wiped out and tired of it all, yes, but never afraid. Sounds crazy, right? But I really wasn't. I love God, and so I trusted him. I believed he was taking care of me, even in the worst of times. I know that he placed people in my life who kept pointing to him.

I especially believe that God answered my prayer to give me a "stronger testimony." Still, I hope I'm through with that, at least for a while. And I hope that I never again go through something as serious as having cancer.

Even though the past two years have been hell, I don't think I would change a thing because I like who I am today. And I am who I am because of all that I've been through.

Mandy Biggs, 16

From Fear To Hope

And we know that in all things God works for the good of those who love him, who have been called according to his purpose.
—**Romans 8:28**

We were "The Three Musketeers Plus One," four teenage girls sitting in a booth at Denny's, talking about everything in the world that came to mind.

My friend, Ann, brought up the subject of God—and how she wondered what he was like. The other two gave their opinions.

I had been a believer all my life. As I sat there listening to them, I remember thinking, *That's not right—God isn't at all like that. He's someone who really cares for us, someone we can know personally.*

For me, he was everything. He was my Father and comforter; my shepherd, teacher and guide; my dearest friend in the world; the one I could go to with all my fears, concerns, needs and desires.

I should say something. I had hardly thought it when an old fear came over me. *What if they ask me questions I can't answer?* And so I sat silently, not entering into the conversation at all. Soon, we moved on to another topic of discussion.

During the next year, several times I had the urge to talk to Ann about the Lord. But each time I chickened out, using the excuse that I didn't know how to witness or that I wouldn't be able to answer any questions she might ask.

In December, a bunch of us, Ann included, went on a weeklong camping trip high up in the snowy mountains near Missoula. The University of Montana sponsored the event and put us up in cabins to learn search-and-rescue and survival skills. Ann and I were together with another girl in one of the smaller cabins.

Throughout the week, I felt that gentle urge to talk to Ann, but still I was afraid that she would ask questions I wouldn't be able to answer. I was afraid of looking stupid if I couldn't explain things and afraid that my ignorance would somehow make her turn away from God instead of bringing her to him. *Lord*, I prayed, *you have lots of people who can say things right. Send her one of them.*

It seemed like a cowardly thing to do, but I felt so inadequate, and I knew there were people, like the camp commander, who were really good at talking about the Lord. I felt that they could do a better job at it than someone like me.

On our last morning there, when Ann and I were alone in the cabin, I had that gentle nudging one last time: *Tell Ann about Me*, came the clear thought.

OK, I'll try, I thought, but then my mind went blank. I couldn't think of a good way to begin, and I let the moment pass. We both headed out for the remaining activities. The campout ended without me ever saying a word to her about the Lord, and we all headed back to Washington.

A couple of months later, Ann was in a horrible car accident. A woman had given her a ride home from her youth meeting one evening. She had been going up the hill that Ann lived on, misjudged the speed of the oncoming traffic, and had tried to turn left into Ann's driveway when suddenly a speeding motorist hit them broadside. It had smashed and torn almost the whole right side of the car away. Ann had been left with serious head and internal injuries. She was in a coma for several days and then died from her injuries.

Oh, Lord, I cried. *No wonder you wanted me to talk to her. And I failed you! What if she didn't find you?*

I was devastated. I had failed the Lord. I had failed Ann, all because I let my stupid fears get in the way.

Never again! I thought as I cut out the newspaper picture of the mangled car from Ann's accident. I pasted it in my scrapbook as a reminder of my failure. *From now on, no matter how frightening it is, somehow I will always try to be a witness when I get the opportunity.*

I read the Bible through to see what it said. I got everything I could find on how to share my faith with others. I got all kinds of training in witnessing and in counseling people who asked for help.

Still, no matter how much I volunteered at my church, or how well I learned to witness, or how many people I led to the Lord, the nagging question was always there: *Had Ann ever found the Lord?*

Dear Lord, please help me to not mess up again. I wanted to be able to say at the end of my life that no matter what happened, I had at least tried.

Almost six years after Ann's death, I was working late one evening at my church when I got a phone call from one of my friends. "Guess what happened to our youth pastor!" she said.

"What?" I asked, only half listening.

"Well, he's been feeling just awful about a kid that he'd been around a lot, but never witnessed to," she said. "Last week the kid was killed in a robbery." Suddenly she had my full attention.

"Our youth pastor always stopped at the local 7-Eleven on his way home from work," she continued. "He said he liked to have coffee and stand around and talk to the clerks. Well, last week one of the clerks was killed in a robbery when the 7-Eleven got held up." I could hear the horror in her voice. "When our pastor heard about it, he suddenly realized that in all the times he'd stopped in there and talked to that very same guy, he'd never once told the clerk that he was a youth pastor or tried to tell the clerk that the Lord loved him.

"He was devastated," she said. "He went around for days feeling just terrible."

I knew exactly how he felt.

"The other day," she continued, "someone asked him, 'Did you hear about the young kid that was killed in that robbery at the 7-Eleven?'"

"When he told her yes, she said, 'Well, the night

before the robbery, he visited such and such church over in Seattle, and he gave his heart to the Lord!'"

My friend told me what a burden had lifted from their youth pastor at hearing that, and how he realized that even though he had failed, God still had a plan in place and had been working on the young man's heart even without the pastor's help.

Thinking about it afterwards, I too had had a huge burden lifted from me. All this time I had subconsciously thought I had been Ann's only hope, but that was foolish. God doesn't work that way. He puts many people and lessons along each pathway. We just need to trust and follow him a step at a time.

Each of us is like one witness in a courtroom. As Peter and John said, "We cannot but speak the things which we have seen and heard."

All that God asks of us is to love the people around us and tell them what he's done in our own lives—how he's loved and comforted us, helped us, and carried us through our trials. Each person adds his own testimony until at some point in time a person hears enough to make that important decision, "Yes, I want God in my life, too."

We each sow individual seeds along the way, sometimes being the first to plant, sometimes watering the seeds, and sometimes being the one to harvest. But all of us have a part, and we can trust in the One who puts all the parts together to make it happen.

Debra K. Matthews

Desires of the Heart

Delight yourself in the Lord and he will give you the desires of your heart.
—Psalms 37:4

As a child, I wanted lots of things. I wanted a bike, and some clothes, and some toys. But there was only one thing that my heart truly desired, and that was my dad.

He left us when I was only a toddler. When I was seven, he came back again for a couple of days, leading us to believe that he wanted to be part of our lives. But he took off, and we never heard from him again. From then on, something inside me yearned for the father that had disappeared.

So I prayed.

Every night I asked God the same thing: "Lord, please bring my dad back into my life." I had always hoped to have that picture-perfect relationship where I would be his little girl, and he would be at all my soccer games and have to approve of my boyfriends—the kinds of things that a caring, involved dad would do.

My mom often told me that there was power in prayer, and she referred me to Psalms 37:4. "Delight yourself in the Lord and he will give you the desires of your heart." It can be easy just to read the words and not comprehend the intended message. You see, the verse does not say wants; it clearly says desires. Now, I wanted a bike and clothes…but I truly desired to have my dad in my life.

Mom also told me that if I prayed from my heart and had faith that God would answer me, then my prayers would be answered.

God did not answer me—at least that's what I thought for a long time. But along the way, I realized that God was not ignoring me. He just answers in three ways: either yes, no, or wait.

As the years went by, it was apparent to me that he was either telling me no or he was telling me to wait. I thought that perhaps my father was no longer alive or that God simply did not want for us to meet.

By the time I turned 19, I had grown up without my dad, but I was still hoping that we could at least have the kind of relationship that meant phone calls, holidays together, and just being more involved in each other's lives. Finally I realized that I would have to lower my expectations of what our relationship could be like, but I did not give up on my prayer.

It was then that God finally granted me the one true desire of my heart.

One day I answered the phone and on the other end was a woman who identified herself as my big sister, Lissa—my father's other daughter. She said that she had been looking for my mom and me for a few years. When she finally did a search for my grandmother's last name, which is unusual, she found her, which led her to us.

Lissa and I had lived together when I was really little, back when Dad was with us. I had some faded memories of those times with her and had thought of her often. Whenever I went out of town for soccer tournaments, I would look in local phone books for my dad's name hoping to find him. I had always looked for Lissa, too. No matter where I went, they were never listed in the book.

I had wanted to try the 1-800-US-SEARCH service, but I didn't have the money to pay for it. At one point I had resorted to writing to Oprah hoping that she would help me, but I never heard back from her. I didn't know until we met again that my sister had written to Oprah too, hoping that she would help her find me.

Lissa and I agreed to meet the following weekend, and it was then that she told me that I had a little sister, Elena, who was 15 and living only 40 miles away from me! Learning that I had another sister was huge. Dad had divorced three times and had daughters by three different women.

I guess I was kind of relieved to find that my dad had not given up on just me—it appeared that he had chosen not to be a father to any of us. When I found out that his mom had left him as a kid, it helped me understand that he had learned this behavior from her.

Then Lissa told me that she knew where my dad was living and how to get in touch with him.

My dream finally had a chance to come true. I was going to connect with my dad at last. Lissa handed me the phone, and I nervously dialed the number. I had to try twice because I was so excited I misdialed the first time. A man answered, and I proceeded to explain to him who I was.

I expected him to be overjoyed to hear from the daughter he hadn't seen in over 12 years. But it turned out to be a weird conversation.

He obviously didn't want to get into anything deep and seemed kind of nervous. We talked about the weather—nothing serious, just small talk. He just kind of joked around about his age—saying that he looked young for 50. He didn't ask many questions about my life, although he did ask about my mom and how she was doing. But then he started getting defensive about how he had left us, and the subject was changed. The call ended without a plan for any reunion.

Even though I was let down by our conversation, I still wanted to meet my dad again. And I really wanted to meet Elena.

A couple of months later, Elena and I got together, and soon after, we flew to Texas to meet Lissa, her kids, and our dad. When I got off the airplane, I saw a little girl peeking around the corner, and I somehow knew instantly that it was Lissa's little girl. I guessed that the woman standing next to her must be my sister.

Dad was supposed to meet us at a nearby restaurant, and when we arrived he was waiting. When he saw me, he walked over to introduce himself. As we faced each other for the first time, it was like looking into a mirror! Every feature was identical—our builds were the same, same eyes, red hair...

But I was also shocked to see a man not like the one he had described on the phone, but one who looked as though he'd lived a hard life.

As I visited with him over the weekend, I got the feeling that I was never really getting a straight story out of him. Again, we didn't get into anything too deep, and so my hope that we would have an ongoing father-daughter relationship began to dwindle. Finally, I was truly forced to lower my expectations of him.

All my life I had assumed that I was ready to meet up with my dad again, but my heavenly Father knew better than I did. If I had been let down again when I was younger and so hopeful that my dad would want to participate in my life, I don't think I could have handled it. Instead of granting my prayer immediately, God waited until it was the right time. He waited until I was mature enough to accept it, because he knew I would be disappointed.

He knew.

As big a disappointment as it was, the visit gave me lots of closure, answered a lot of questions for me, and gave me the chance to have a relationship with my sisters, which has been worth it all.

So, in the end, all those bedtime prayers I said were not useless. God showed me that he does answer our prayers, and he gives us the desires of our hearts—when we're ready. We just need to continue praying and never give up faith that he will answer.

Tracy Simmons

That Infamous Semester

"For I am the Lord, your God, who takes hold of your right hand and says to you, Do not fear; I will help you."
—**Isaiah 41:13**

Spring of my freshman year in college was probably the most difficult season of my life thus far. There were times when I would just lie in my dorm room in bewilderment of why bad things kept happening to me, and there were other days when I had enough faith to shut off my alarm and crawl out of bed to face one more day.

Things got off to a rocky start since I was a transfer student, and jumping into the mix of a whole new student body was quite unnerving. When I began college, I never envisioned myself attending more than one institution, but God had other plans. At the time I couldn't understand the significance of my transfer and sometimes questioned if I had made the right decision.

The first blow to my semi-smooth flowing life happened the first week of classes. I was standing during praise and worship time when all of a sudden my vision blurred and I began seeing black spots. I figured it would go away, but instead I became nauseated. Then my vision started to disappear completely. I felt my way out of the auditorium, stumbling as I went. I couldn't see a thing, and my body was ice-cold as well as drenched in sweat.

After about 15 minutes my vision came back, and I was able to get to my dorm room to call my mom. She scheduled an appointment with our family doctor, who took some X-rays and then instructed me to see a neurosurgeon. The neurosurgeon ordered a spinal tap, which was pretty scary-sounding. On top of that, ironically and inconveniently, the spinal tap was scheduled for the same day my mom was going in for surgery. My dad ended up running back and forth between two hospitals and actually took my mom to the wrong hospital that morning because he was so stressed out. The neurosurgeon determined I needed a spinal fusion and bone graft surgery.

Then in the middle of April, one month after the dreaded spinal tap, I began experiencing severe pain in my jaw. I went to see the dentist, only to discover that all four of my wisdom teeth were impacted in my jaw and needed to come out as soon as possible. I had the excruciating experience of having my wisdom teeth yanked out while I was awaiting the other surgery.

The surgery was scheduled to be right after the spring semester, which killed my summer plans of going on a mission trip to Europe. Instead, I'd be out of commission for the entire summer while I spent ten weeks in a full-body back brace, followed by physical therapy for several months.

Needless to say, I was feeling pretty crappy altogether. I just kept asking myself why God was doing this to me and found myself constantly on guard for the next crippling blow that might come my way.

But that's not how the whole thing played out. I felt about as helpless as I can imagine ever feeling, but I kept my sanity, because I continually depended on God. I finally stopped asking "why" and decided to roll with it. My attitude changed, and I found that even when I was too tired or angry to "feel" God, I still knew he was there.

Sometimes I would be at my wits' end, drained of tears, and I would just experience an overwhelming peace that allowed me to rest.

Now I believe that when we go through our own valleys of utter darkness, God will reassure us that he is the only thing constant and unchanging in our lives. In the process, he brings things to light that we wouldn't ordinarily notice or appreciate. Even the smallest kindnesses that friends and family show us tend to be much more appreciated during a low point.

I received cards from friends and even people I didn't know well saying, "I'm praying for you," or with an uplifting Bible verse that helped point me back to the Ultimate Comforter. There were roses and a cake from new friends, a roommate who offered hugs when I couldn't take it anymore, a boyfriend who brought ice cream to soothe an aching jaw, and a special aunt who pampered me endlessly and took me out to lunch and shopping even though I looked like a walking lightning rod in my back brace.

There was my dad, who drove me carefully home from the hospital, ignoring impatient drivers who were hovering on the verge of road rage and avoiding all those infamous county road potholes. There was my grandma who dressed and bathed me, church members who showered me with get-well cards, and my ever-supportive family, always willing to take me out for a walk when I moved slower than a snail and could only make it a few hundred feet.

All the while there was my amazing mother, who stayed up all night trying to keep me comfortable through muscle spasms and medication complications; who sat by my bedside and read to me when my vision was too blurred to read; who dressed me, showered me (donning a raincoat and climbing in the shower with me), put on my socks, and tied my shoes. She bent over backwards (sometimes literally) to meet my needs.

All these little blessings have become memories I now carry with me for the rest of my life—memories that I can break out and relive when my world seems to be a bit dark and out of control.

Now, instead of looking back on my surgeries and thinking of the pain and the discomfort, I think about all the people who love me and expressed it so generously and selflessly. I think about the sacrifices made and the genuine concern that was shown to me.

I remember questioning God over and over, asking, "Why me?" I couldn't understand why I had to go to a college so much closer to home and then got slammed with one painful experience after another. But had I not been so close, I would have had many more complications in dealing with all the struggles that came my way that infamous semester.

I now realize that stuff happens to everyone, but when you have God in your life, he provides you with everything and everyone you need to get through the tough times.

If all of this hadn't happened, I would never have realized how much I am loved.

What a gift.

Kristen Funk, 19

Paid in Full

"Pray that the Lord your God will tell us where we should go and what we should do."
—Jeremiah 42:3

Sometimes being obedient to God can get pretty challenging. I'd been dating a girl, and the relationship was getting a little out of control, even though I knew it wasn't really right for me.

Getting so caught up with this girl made it hard for me to keep God in first place. At one point, things were really deteriorating, and I began praying for direction. My answer came in a phone call from my pastor, Mike Macintosh, from Horizon Church.

Mike called and offered me a gig as drummer with his band that did Beatles covers. It would be a mini-tour for two weeks. I knew the bass player, which made the offer even better, so it seemed like an answer to prayer. I really needed to get away and try to sort out everything that was going on with my girlfriend.

When I took the gig, I never asked my pastor or the other band members about money. I thought I was going on the tour as an opportunity to get closer to God.

One night I was hanging around in the hotel room with my bass player friend, who was rooming with me on the tour. We started talking about how people become the Billy Grahams of the world—really great and amazing teachers. We were saying, "Wow. How does that happen?" In the middle of the conversation, I distinctly heard God speak to my heart. He said that those great in ministry were faithful in the little things. This stayed on my heart while I was trying to fall asleep. I tossed and turned all night.

Finally, at about four a.m., I fell asleep and had a dream. It was so real that it stuck with me the whole next day like a really important thing you know you have to remember or do something about.

In the dream, God was telling me that I was going to go to a Bible college to learn more about his word and that my pastor was going to pay for it.

The next morning, I kept thinking, *That so was weird.* I didn't know what to make of it, so I didn't say anything about it to my friend. But it was so heavy on my mind and heart, I just prayed about it through the day and talked to God about it whenever it came to mind, saying, "That was pretty random, God, but you know, whatever."

After we got back from the tour, I broke things off with my girlfriend. It seemed like that was what I really needed to do. It was hard, but looking back, it freed me up to be available for God's plan for my life. With nothing else to distract me from God's will, I prayed for direction and waited patiently for his reply.

One Sunday, not long after we came back from the tour, I was sitting in church when someone made an announcement about a Bible college that was offering a nine-week course that was beginning soon. It sounded like a great opportunity until I heard how much it cost. The tuition was about four grand—way over my head. Since my parents weren't Christians, I couldn't really ask them to help. Even though I felt led to go, I didn't have a clue about how I could pay for it.

Well, I ended up at the course orientation, just to check it out. I didn't have to make a commitment. It seemed like an amazing course, and I was more interested than ever. But with the cost of tuition, I didn't think there was a chance that I'd be able to go. So, again, I prayed about it. If it were meant to be, then God would make it happen.

About a week before the course was to start, out of the blue, a check for $1500 came in the mail. It had been signed by my pastor, Mike, from Horizon Church. I was like, "What? He must have put too many zeros on this check!" So I called Mike and said, "Hey, you paid me too much!"

"We didn't pay you too much," he firmly replied. "You're a professional drummer, and you deserve to be paid like one. There's no mistake."

I knew immediately that the check was God's answer to my prayers and would be the down payment for the course. I thanked Mike, got off the phone, and headed straight to the bank. I cashed the check, took the money to the college, and enrolled. Then, on faith, I just trusted that God would take care of the rest.

My classes ran Monday through Friday, so I was either in class or studying like crazy in between. Because of the course, I wasn't making much money, since weekends were the only time I had off. But every few weeks, I would get a call from Mike, asking me to play a gig. Each call would come like clockwork, just about the time I needed to make a tuition payment. It was incredible. Every time I needed money, I'd get a check in the mail—signed by Mike Macintosh. I knew that it was meant for my tuition, and I never missed a payment.

By the time the course was over, I had my tuition paid in full with checks signed by none other than my pastor, Mike Macintosh.

Even though I earned it, Mike provided the work and ultimately the money I needed to go to Bible College. Pretty wild.

Then, in a weird coincidence, Mike was asked to speak at the graduation. It was after the ceremony that I finally told him about the dream. He smiled and shook his head, amused at the way God works. Although he was grateful to help God fulfill his plan for me, it blew him away that he never had a clue that he was even doing it.

God has some amazing ways of getting through to us and making sure that our destinies are fulfilled.

Since then, I pay more attention to my dreams.

Aaron Redfield

03

He is a God of
Mighty Power

"Lift your eyes and look to the heavens: Who created all these? He who brings out the starry host one by one, and calls them each by name. Because of his great power and mighty strength, not one of them is missing."
—Isaiah 40:26

"They will tell of the power of your awesome works, and I will proclaim your great deeds."
—Psalms 145:6

"You are the God who performs miracles; you display your power among the peoples."
—Psalms 77:14

The Door's Open

It makes no difference who you are or where you're from--if you want God and are ready to do as he says, the door is open.
—Acts 10:35, The Message

"If you're just hanging out, I might as well put you to work. Here, Rory, I'll give you a couple of bucks if you take this broom and sweep up around here," I suggest to the kid as he sits on the counter thumbing through a catalog.

I'm not sure he knows exactly why he's here or what he's looking for, so I take him under my wing, so to speak. I remember what it was like. Being from a broken home, wanting to be somewhere hip, where you felt you could belong. Where the door was open.

I've been letting him hang around the shop and have even taken him to church on Sundays, often springing for lunch afterward.

When I was around his age, in my early teens, my parents were going through a divorce. I felt like the world had slammed the door in my face, so I looked up to the only person available to me: my big brother. He and his friends were into punk and rockabilly music. The whole scene—their music, their tattoos, the drugs—it all fascinated me.

I escaped into this image and got into drugs pretty heavily. My thing was to be against everything, to be a rebel. I pretty much took whatever drugs I could get my hands on. Then, after the divorce happened, I just didn't care anymore, to a point when I wanted to destroy my life. I know my parents cared about me, but I didn't care about my life. I just wanted to push it to the edge, to the extreme. I did as many drugs as I could without overdosing.

When I was 14, I got a paper delivery job after school to get the stuff I wanted. My whole paycheck went to buying drugs. Sometimes I would show up at school or do my route on acid.

The one good thing that I was into was skateboarding. I had talent, but I never had the desire to compete. I just did it for the love of it. I probably would have gotten tossed out for doing drugs anyway.

My schoolwork went south, and I was headed toward getting F's in all my classes. But before the grading period was over, I went to the teacher, found out what I could do to get a passing grade, and crammed something together. I ended up barely passing.

By the time I started high school I was really depressed. I was living to do drugs, skate, and buy whatever I wanted with the money I was making.

One day, three of my friends were over, and we were crossing different types of acid to make our high more interesting. We were tripping really hard when my friend, Bill, started losing touch with reality. He didn't know what was real and what was fake—what you would call a bad trip. He would snap from being violent, to loving, to crying, to laughter. We were all trying to calm him down when a car accident happened right in front of my house. This made him trip even more—he thought that one of us had died, and he was freaking out.

He started saying stuff about wanting to go towards the light and kept trying to get close to the lamps in the house. At one point, he tried to grab on to a light bulb and burned himself, so we turned off all the lights in the room. Bill was standing in front of our plate glass window when he saw the streetlight. Before anyone could stop him, he chucked my skateboard through the huge glass pane and tried to pull himself through the window. He cut his arms up and down on the glass all the way to the arteries. He was bleeding so badly that with every heartbeat, blood was shooting out of his veins.

The cops came. They called an ambulance that took Bill to the hospital. While he was recovering, a youth pastor came by to counsel him, and as a result, he accepted Christ into his life.

You might think that the whole experience made me change my ways and clean up my act. But at that point, Bill and I split, because I kept on using drugs.

I started a new job and was bringing in pretty good money for a 16-year-old. I had money at the end of each week to buy pretty much anything I wanted. After a while, I started wondering what life was about: getting rich, sleeping with girls, doing drugs? What was it really about? I began to think that if this was it, then it was pretty stupid. It was a big waste of time.

I was constantly questioning the meaning of life. Then out of the blue, I thought, *Hey, I'm gonna go check out church.* I had gone to church when I was younger with my parents for Easter and Christmas.

I stopped into a church down the street from my house the following Sunday. The message made me feel like my soul was being fed—like my spirit was being replenished. I kept going back on Sundays and would come out feeling pretty good. But then I would go do drugs again all week, and I would feel like junk again. Soon, drugs began to leave me feeling empty, like my soul was dead.

Then one day, my old friend Bill called me. It must have been the Lord that made him call me, because we hadn't seen each other in a long time. He invited me to his church and was surprised when I told him that I had been going to church, too.

We went to his church together, and the third time I went, the pastor was giving a sermon that seemed to be talking about my life. I had never met him, and my friend had never told him anything about me, but he was speaking to me as if he were looking straight at me. I turned to my friend and said, "Dude, he's looking right at me," and Bill turned to me and said, "Dude, he's not." But I knew God was looking at me through the pastor—God was talking through that man, saying, "This is your call. I'm calling you out right now. Give your life to me." The pastor did an altar call, and by that time I was in tears. I gave my life to the Lord that day.

After that I did a complete 180 and have never looked back.

One day, right after the altar call, I was cleaning up and going through stuff in my desk that I didn't want anymore. I came across a picture that I had put in an old wallet. It was a picture of the cross between two hands with a Bible underneath. I tucked it away, thinking to myself that I wanted to have this tattooed on me someday. I knew a skinhead that did tattooing in his garage, so I looked him up, and he did it for me.

I didn't know it then, but that was the beginning of my life's calling.

I had always been the kind of kid who draws on everything. I constantly doodled in school. In high school, I put some of my drawings on T-shirts to make my own unique statement. After I got the tattoo, I started drawing again, but this time I was designing tattoos. The whole process interested me and I ended up getting my own cheap tattoo kit. I started by tattooing my leg, but I ended up with a really bad infection. Nurse Mom pulled out the science books and had me study up on the process of sterilization.

My friends found out that I had a kit and started asking me to tattoo them. Before I knew it, I had a following.

But I had a problem. The little kit I had was totally inadequate, and I needed better equipment if I was going to do justice to my customers and my designs. My colors weren't good, and the needles weren't great quality, which reflected in the end result. It was frustrating, because the profession is so tightly controlled that you can't get the top equipment or even the names of companies that sell it.

So I prayed to God. "I'll give it a month, Lord, and if I don't have a lead or the equipment within a month, I am quitting." I figured that if he really wanted me to be doing this, he'd come up with a way for me to get the goods.

Within a month, through weird serendipity, I found a guy who worked for a tattoo equipment company. I called and his wife happened to be there that day. We just hit it off. Usually, you have to send in your license and business card, but by the end of the conversation she asked, "What do you need?" She didn't ask me for any proof of anything. I got everything right away. I said, "Okay, Lord, you answered me, so I'll keep doing this."

I started getting a reputation, and even people at other tattoo shops knew my work.

I set up a tattoo studio in my little house. I got so busy that I finally quit my job to tattoo full-time. I was a Christian, but most of my friends were still punks. The punk scene really took off, and I started tattooing tons of guys from the local punk bands. Soon I had bikers and all kinds of interesting but total strangers in my house getting tattooed. I tried tattooing in other shops, but it was hard, because the tattoo industry has a lot of junk going on behind the scenes—porn, drugs, sex, gangs—and I couldn't work in these places. One after another, I'd leave and never go back.

One day, a guy named Rob called me. He had gotten one of my cards, and the card had a fish on it, which symbolized Christianity. He said he didn't know you could be a Christian and get a tattoo. "I wanted to let you know that I gave my life to the Lord, and it's because of your business card and that fish that I did it," he told me on the phone. I was blown away that my mere business card could minister to a guy like that. I knew it was the Lord who did the work. That was only the beginning.

Two years later, I was finally getting my own shop together, and I was almost ready to open. I hadn't talked to Rob since that phone call, but someone told me about a guy who had lost his job because he had secretly added a fish in someone's satanic tattoo. It was Rob.

As you might have guessed, he came to work for me. He's putting tattoos for God on people every day now—only now they're requesting them.

We have ministered to countless people from our shop, and many people have gotten saved there. People walk in and say, "It's different here; it's a good vibe here." I tell them it's because the Holy Spirit is there. It's because we are all Christians. To say the least, it's a different atmosphere from other tattoo shops.

Word got out about us through the punk and then the Christian music scene. Then the international media covered our story. Now people come to my shop from all over the world as a sort of pilgrimage to get tattooed for the Lord.

I love tattoos. I love seeing them on people's bodies, and I love seeing them on my own body. But tattooing is a permanent thing; it's a commitment. If you ever consider getting one, you'd better get something that you know you're going to love for the rest of your life—and God is a great thing to love for the rest of your life.

I always hear my customers say how they use their tattoos as witnessing tools. They open up conversation with all kinds of people. That's definite proof that God has used my passion to open doors—a thousand doors. And he keeps on opening them.

Now we've expanded the shop to include a ministry in the building next door. We have Bible studies there almost every night. Each month God has provided the rent to keep it open.

It's another day at the shop. I'm covering a swastika on a skinhead-turned-Christian when I see Rory coming up the driveway to hang out for another day.

I think about his life and smile, realizing that with God, anything is possible.

"Come on in, Rory," I call to him. "The door's open."

Sid Stankovits

The Phone Call

And this is love: that we walk in obedience to his commands...
—2 John 1:6

I hadn't seen or talked to Dwayne for about a year. We had been young adult ministry interns at the same church in San Diego, California, when my life took a turn in a new direction and I relocated to Costa Mesa, about 100 miles away.

The year before I left San Diego, Dwayne had gone to a speaking engagement when, out of nowhere, he suddenly collapsed in a seizure. When they figured out what had happened, the news was about as bad as it could be. Dwayne had a massive brain tumor. He immediately underwent surgery, but the doctors weren't able to get the whole tumor. He was still struggling with the cancer when I moved and lost track of him.

One particular morning, I got up feeling very lonely and discouraged. I was really missing my friends back home and was depressed. I felt like crying. Moping around the house, I wasn't much in the mood to have my usual quiet time with the Lord, which I did every morning. I decided to call a friend in San Diego to whine and complain.

I picked up the phone and felt an urgency in my heart to have a quiet time. I remember reasoning in my head that I was going to make this phone call first. But the feeling was so strong that I answered out loud, "*Okay!*" and hung up the phone as it was ringing through to the other end.

I plopped myself on the couch and wasn't sure where to start but sensed that I was supposed to open up to Philippians 1. I started reading the letter from Paul about how even as he was in chains, he was glad that his life was being used for the glory of Christ. I read the part where he says that "Christ will be exalted in my body, whether by life or by death. For to me, to live is Christ and to die is gain."

As I read, I felt a heaviness on my heart, and then I just starting sobbing. Suddenly, an image of Dwayne came into my mind, and I just started praying for him. Now, this came out of nowhere—I hadn't seen or talked to Dwayne for about a year.

I must have prayed for him for over half an hour. I don't even remember all the things that I prayed for him, because it was as if the Lord were directing the prayer the whole time. I was just standing in the gap for Dwayne praying for courage and thanking God for him. The whole time, my heart felt like it had a brick on it. I was sobbing and sobbing as I was praying for him—it was so intense. It was kind of a supernatural experience, because it felt like I was praying as if *I* were Dwayne.

I had started the quiet time at around 9:00, and it was around 10:30 when I finished. But then I heard the Lord saying, "Call Dwayne."

I was totally overwhelmed and thought, *No way am I going to call him! I have no idea what to say, and who am I anyway to call him and say anything about his cancer? I don't have cancer, so I don't know what he's going through or where he is with it right now.*

I sat there arguing and reasoning with God, fighting the message that I should call Dwayne. Finally, I felt so completely disobedient telling God that I wasn't going to call him, that I began thinking about how I could reach him. Since it was a weekday, I figured that he would be at work.

I called the church where we had worked, and they told me that he was out for the morning. I hung up and said to myself, *See—he's not even there.*

That afternoon he returned my call. At first he seemed really distant and asked why I was calling him. He said, "What's up?"

I was so freaked out that my whole body started shaking, and I began rattling, "I don't know—nothing's happened to me like this before, but you were on my heart this morning, and I was reading scripture, and I felt like I was supposed to be praying for you." I took a big breath and continued to get it all out. "I feel like I have a word from the Lord for you, but if this is not from God, then I just ask your forgiveness ahead of time." My voice was shaking, and I started crying. I felt foolish, like he was going to think I was totally whacked.

I got silent for a while as I tried to gain composure. Finally I asked, "Is this okay?" He seemed a little distant or apprehensive, but he answered, "Yeah, it's okay."

So I said, "Here it goes." I read all of Philippians 1 and just broke it down for him like God had shown it to me. As I went, I took each passage and told him what God said to me in relation to his cancer.

"Your cancer is like Paul being in chains for the gospel. These chains can have a purpose—this cancer can be used as part of God's plan. Don't be discouraged, because you will have an audience that would never otherwise know the truth of Christ. Because you've been given a gift of communicating God's truth, he is using this. You're not going to die from it; God will use you. It's because of your faithfulness and God's blessing that it can happen."

That's when I started apologizing again, saying, "I don't have cancer. I can't even fathom how painful it is, and I am so sorry. If this is not of the Lord, you can just stop me right now."

He was silent on the other end, and so I just finished what I felt I was supposed to say by sharing verse 12, which talks about how Paul felt he was put in his situation for the purpose of spreading the gospel. Then I shared verse 20, which affirmed that Dwayne could exalt Christ as he shared his experience.

Then I was quiet and sat there crying as I waited for Dwayne to respond.

"And what time was this?" he firmly asked.

"Around nine or so," I meekly answered. "I finished around 10:30."

"Do you know where I was at nine o'clock this morning?"

"Nooo," I tearfully answered back.

"I was in my bed," he continued. "I couldn't get up because I was in so much pain. I was crying out to God in despair and contemplating how I could die. I just wanted to die right then," he admitted.

Then he told me that at that exact time, he was also journaling his thoughts and prayers to God. He grabbed his journal and began to read to me what he had written that morning at the same time that I was crying out to God on his behalf.

"'God have mercy on me,'" he read, "'and tell me why you have allowed this to happen? What is your purpose for me? Why do I have cancer? You have to give me some direction. You have to give me some hope, God!'"

He shared with me all that he had written in his journal at the moment that I was praying for him. It was apparent that not only was God giving me words for Dwayne at that time, but God was also using me to burden-bear with him as I was weeping and praying—helping him to carry his pain and sorrow—knowing that it was too heavy for Dwayne to hold in that moment.

I wondered why God would use someone like me who was 100 miles away and didn't have a strong connection to Dwayne—somebody out of the blue who was clueless to his situation.

The answer was clear.

If it had been a person who knew what Dwayne was going through, it would not have been as obvious that God was the one speaking through the situation.

Dwayne knew that I had no idea what he'd been going through.

We both sat there for a moment with chills, just marveling at what God had just done.

The next thing out of Dwayne's mouth, though, topped off the whole experience. It was as if a bright light went off in his head. I think he was discovering the significance of what he was saying as the words came slowly from his mouth.

"This is the exact scripture that God gave to me when I was diagnosed with the brain tumor," he said.

He flipped his Bible open to Philippians and there, noted to the side of the passages that I read to him, was a date from the time when he was told he had cancer.

Now, almost two years later, on this day when he had cried out to God wanting to die, I had been used to lead him back to the scripture God had given him when his illness had begun.

"God already told me a long time ago that this could be used for his purpose, but I forgot," he confessed. He seemed blown away.

Through the conversation we had, God was again reminding him that he had never forgotten him nor forsaken him. It was a great illustration of how God is consistent. It was like he was saying to Dwayne, "Remember? I told you!"

"Thank you so much for obeying God's voice," Dwayne said softly and emphatically. "If you hadn't listened to God speaking and called me, I would have never gotten the answer from him that I needed."

Dwayne got his direction from the Lord, and as for me, I got the incredible experience of being used by God. Although I hadn't been in the mood and at first had been stubborn, I had still listened to God speaking to me, and he honored that. What a huge lesson and an amazing blessing for me.

As we closed the conversation I noticed that Dwayne's demeanor had dramatically changed from when the call began. He seemed to have a spark in him that I hadn't heard in his voice until now.

"I've been asked to speak at a conference this month for cancer patients," he told me. "Some of them know Christ, but a lot of them don't."

His audience that would never otherwise know Christ, I thought.

Then he vowed, "And I'm going to share the gospel— boldly."

And he did.

And he still is today.

And the last I heard, he is cancer-free.

Jennifer Briner

Now I want you to know, brothers, that what has happened to me has really served to advance the gospel. As a result, it has become clear throughout the whole palace guard and to everyone else that I am in chains for Christ. Because of my chains, most of the brothers in the Lord have been encouraged to speak the word of God more courageously and fearlessly... I eagerly expect and hope that I will in no way be ashamed, but will have sufficient courage so that now as always Christ will be exalted in my body, whether by life or by death. For to me, to live is Christ and to die is gain.
—Philippians 1:12-14 and 20-21

Building Blocks

If we are faithless, he will remain faithful, for he cannot disown himself.
—2 Timothy 2:13

Just after our first record came out, it seemed like my faith was going in circles. I was really doubting God and questioning everything. There I was, out there representing God through music, while having lots of questions and rethinking my beliefs. I was restless.

Around that time, we took a trip to Daytona Beach, Florida, to a Christian conference. On the last day, I heard God speak to my heart. It was as though he were telling me to prepare myself, because I was going to be talking to some people later on that day. It was a definite feeling in my heart. I responded by saying, "Lord, if this is you, make it so."

Later that night, after the conference was over, a group of us went out to Denny's at about two in the morning. An hour later we went down to the beach. I was just sitting there playing my guitar when two guys came walking up the beach toward me. They began talking to me—just kind of shooting the breeze. It became obvious that one of them was kind of drunk. Pretty soon, for whatever reason, they both started sharing about their personal lives. One of the guys told me that he was leaving to go into the military and that it was his last weekend to party with his friends.

Then, out of nowhere, the conversation turned to the topic of God. We ended up spending more than three hours talking about God's character and what it means to believe in Jesus. Eventually, we ended up in the lobby of a hotel near where we'd been sitting. A hotel employee finally came along and told us that we had to leave because we weren't staying there.

We wrapped things up, said our goodbyes, and parted ways. I was headed in the direction of my hotel when I heard someone call my name. I turned to see the two guys running toward me. *What are they doing?* I thought to myself. I headed toward them not really knowing what to expect. When we reached each other, one of them said to me, "We want to accept Christ. Right now. Can you help us do that?"

At some point in our early morning conversation, they had shared with me how years before, they'd both gone to a Christian conference, but they hadn't accepted God. Now, as the sun began to rise over the ocean, they stood there asking me to help them accept Christ into their lives.

The crazy thing was, as I helped them find their faith, I rediscovered mine as well. All of my questions about whether or not God is real, or hears us, or cares at all, were answered.

God helped me reconfirm my faith when he spoke to my heart and then followed through with his message. It became a landmark building block of faith for me. He is so merciful and loving, he chose to love me through my time of doubt by gifting me with an experience that made it evident that he is undeniably real.

Phillip LaRue

Overnight

My message and my preaching were not with wise and persuasive words, but with a demonstration of the Spirit's power, so that your faith might not rest on men's wisdom, but on God's power.
—1 **Corinthians 2:4-5**

Walking around the house with one of her cigarettes hanging out of my mouth usually worked pretty well. More often than not, I'd get the attention that I craved from my mom, once she caught on.

She had smoked for as long as I could remember, and by the time I was 11, I not only knew that messing with her cigarettes was a way to push her buttons, I was also curious about how smoking worked—what they tasted like and if they made you feel more grown up. For a few years, she would laugh at me and shake her head, playing a kind of cat and mouse game with me until I gave up the cigarette that I had playfully pulled from her pack of Marlboros.

Then, one day when I was 12, she handed me a cigarette and allowed me to light it up.

I started smoking.

I shared cigarettes with my mom, smoking around the house after school. Soon I began to befriend other kids who smoked, and for some reason, it was easy to sneak around the campus and bathrooms at my school to take a few puffs in between classes. By eighth grade, I *needed* these cigarette breaks. Smoking had become a habit—I was addicted. It was no longer a choice.

One day, there was an assembly at our junior high school which featured a guy who had cancer of the throat. It was pretty eerie to hear him speak. He had to talk through a speaker in his throat because he had lost the use of his vocal cords. In this electric-sounding, monotone type of voice, he tried to warn my friends and me to stop smoking so that we wouldn't turn out like him. I remember thinking to myself, *I will never be like that!*

Then later that year my grandpa died of lung cancer. I dealt with it by telling myself that I needed to smoke more to deal with his death. Weird logic, huh? But smoking had become a crutch, and I used the excuse that it comforted me.

By the time I was 17, in my junior year of high school, I was smoking a pack and a half a day. It was also then that I decided I wanted to be a lifeguard. So I tried to quit smoking.

It was hard.

I *couldn't* do it.

I figured then that I would always be a smoker, because it was just impossible for me to quit. I was able to cut down, but I couldn't cut it completely out of my life. So I told everyone that I had a terrible fear of diving as an excuse not to get certified as a lifeguard. Deep down I knew that I didn't have the endurance to save a drowning life.

Around that time, a friend invited me to come with her to her church youth group. I had been there a few times as a fifth grader, but now I was in high school, full of a past that I wondered if people could see as I walked into the room. But when I looked at the teens in the youth group, they smiled and seemed too preoccupied with being happy to notice anything negative about me.

The meeting was pretty fun overall until it came time for what they called "confession." There I was, feeling kind of trapped, knowing that my turn would come around. When it came, I felt like there was a huge, hot spotlight shining on me. At the last minute, I came up with something to say. Some of the teens in the youth group knew I smoked, so I decided to just use that as something to confess.

"I smoke a pack a day," I divulged.

I felt that if these positive, happy people knew I smoked a pack and a half a day, it might rock their world too much. Little did I know that the One it mattered to the most already knew how much I smoked and how much I lied about it. But what did I know about anything like that? I wasn't a Christian—I was a partyer! I decided that I shouldn't dare confess any of the other illegal stuff I smoked.

In reply to my confession, the youth pastor asked me, "Do you believe that God can heal you from the addiction of smoking?" I really wasn't expecting him to throw such a question at me, so I sat there thinking for a minute. Finally, I thought to myself, *it's worth a shot, I've tried everything else*, and so I responded, "Yeah. Sure."

Looking back now, I realize that I was just testing the reality of God. The group prayed for him to break me from the addiction of smoking, and in the prayer, they prayed that I would have the strength to go home and throw my cigarettes and lighter away.

The next morning, I woke up nauseated at the smell of smoke from my mom's cigarette burning. I was shocked. How could this be? I actually tried to smoke, but it made me sick to my stomach. *Me*—the pack-and-a-half-a-day girl could no longer stand even the smell of smoke.

Not possible.

Unreal.

I could no longer imagine having the desire to smoke. In some weird way, I had the feeling that I had never even lit a cigarette before! There was just no way that I could have made this change on my own after five years of smoking every day. It was definitely a God thing. He had *definitely* done a modern-day miracle in my life.

In a way, I felt like my image was shot. I had thought it was cool to be a smoker. It was a status thing. But eventually I gave up smoking other things, too, because it didn't make sense to me to do one and not the other. Besides, I had completely lost the craving for smoking *anything*.

It took some coming around, but I also finally decided to ask God into my life. It wasn't easy at first. Slowly but surely I realized that some of the things I had been holding on to really didn't compare to what I got from being in a relationship with God.

It's true that the truth will set you free, and the truth is this: he is a powerful, loving God who answers prayers and changes lives.

He changed mine overnight.

Renee Krapf

Michael's Gift

Therefore let everyone who is godly pray to you while you may be found; surely when the mighty waters rise, they will not reach him.
—**Psalms 32:6**

Michael is the third of four children in my family. My mom and dad have told me that there were some extraordinary circumstances surrounding the conception and birth of my brother, so I've never been surprised at all the things Michael has done in his short life. But I am constantly amazed at God's plan for him.

We started to observe special things about Michael when he was about two. One time, in the midst of a severe drought in Texas where we live, we were all praying for rain. Michael happened to overhear us, and the next time we were in church, he told my dad that he had asked Jesus to make rain fall on our house that day. My dad smiled at Michael and said, "Okay, Michael, but there is not one cloud in the sky." Within an hour after church, a small cluster of clouds formed directly over our house and showered us with wonderful rain. I think that's when we first gained an insight into Michael's ability to connect with God.

Another time, we had a car that just started to die for no reason. My mom could be driving 60 mph or just pulling around the block; it didn't matter. It would just die. We'd have to wait indefinitely before it would start again. It was pretty embarrassing.

On one such occasion, the whole family was there in the car, and we had an important appointment to keep. Of course, the car died. Michael, who was busy keeping himself amused in the backseat, was clueless as to why we had stopped. He seemed more intent on playing than noticing whether the car was moving. My dad tried to start the car, over and over, with no luck. After the eighth or ninth unsuccessful attempt, Michael popped up from the back seat and announced that he would ask Jesus to help the car to start—that minute. He said the prayer, and Daddy turned the key. I'm sure you know what happened. We all had an incredible feeling of gratitude, grace, and inspiration that day. Michael just smiled.

I tell these two stories to prepare you for the one that, without any doubt, will remain in my heart forever.

It was a Saturday in October when rain began to fall in our hometown of Luling. My parents had taken my siblings and me to our grandparents' house because they had a business trip planned to Fort Worth. They left before dawn, just as the rain was beginning to fall in thick sheets from the sky. All of south central Texas was experiencing torrential downpours of the same magnitude. Austin was already flooding by the time my parents traveled through on their way to Fort Worth.

They finished their business late in the day and began their journey home. Although they were tempted to drive part of the way and spend the night in a hotel because it was getting late, something told them to go home. When they tried calling us, they couldn't get through. Then their unsuccessful attempts to reach any phone numbers in our town began to alarm them. All phone lines in our area were down due to the flooding.

Half an hour before my parents reached home, they crossed the bridge in San Marcos only to find that the river had risen so high that it was now tightly hugging the trestles below the cement bridge. They were shocked. My dad hadn't seen the river that high in 25 years. They hurried to get home, unprepared for the horrors that lay ahead. Upon arriving at home, everything seemed to be intact. It was well after 2:00 a.m., so they went to bed, only to be awakened by someone banging at the door three hours later.

Dad answered the door to a policeman who was evacuating our neighborhood. He told my dad that they had to get out right away because the river had risen to an all-time high and had pushed the creeks over their bounds. This was causing severe flooding in places that had never flooded before, and the water was due to rise another nine to 12 feet in our neighborhood.

Another nine to 12 feet would surely flood our home. Six houses to our left had already flooded, and two were almost completely under water. My mom and dad ran to look outside. The water had covered more than two-thirds of the back yard.

Immediately they raced to grab our family photos and some other memorabilia. Next, they took their business equipment out. They continued to load up as the water kept rising and rising.

After trying again and again, my mom finally got through to my grandparents' house around 6:45 a.m. and let them know that our house was expected to flood. As dawn began to break, the brownish-green floodwaters had engulfed the pool and our entire back yard and were rising to the door. The water had overtaken two more houses to our left and one to our right. The rising floodwaters were creeping straight toward our house.

Around 9:00 a.m., my mom got through again to my grandparents. This time she sounded desperate. She asked my granddad to please wake Michael, explain to him what was happening, and ask him to ask Jesus to spare our home. She confided in my granddad that it looked inevitable that we would lose our home, but because she truly believed in Michael's special connection, it was worth a try.

My mom got off the phone and went to her room, which was closest to the floodwaters. She opened the big windows that allowed her to see the surge of water pushing in. It was already at the window ledge and less than an inch from penetrating our home.

This is what happened next.

As if someone had flipped a light switch, the wind started to blow strongly from a northerly direction, literally pushing the water back from the house and moving it across our yard. I remember my mother saying that she knew in that instant that Michael's prayer had been answered.

I occasionally look at the pictures my parents took of the flood. The water came all the way up and around three sides of our home, but never, never came in. Eight houses on our left and two houses on our right had been taken. But our house, in the middle of others that had gone under, remained untouched.

It wasn't as if we were the only ones that noticed the miracle that happened that day. People from volunteer clean-up crews, neighbors, and friends went on and on about how lucky we were. They could not believe how the water missed us. It didn't make any sense, they said.

Well, it made perfect sense to our family. We had many times before witnessed God's responses to the prayers of an undoubting, innocent little kid—my amazing brother Michael.

Chelsea Rollert, 15

Perfect Waves

He performs wonders that cannot be fathomed, miracles that cannot be counted.
—Job 5:9

My only dream in life was to be a professional surfer. I loved baseball and other sports, but I had quit all of them by the seventh grade to focus on surfing. All through junior high and high school I did everything and anything to reach the pro level: I surfed every chance I got and competed in every amateur contest I could enter. I needed a big break, but no matter what I did, it still seemed far from happening.

In my junior year of high school, a weird thing started to happen. Night after night, after partying with my friends, I'd come home thinking, *I don't even enjoy this.* I felt empty. I'd end up crying myself to sleep. I thought, *Why am I crying? There's nothing wrong with my life. What's my problem?* Everything the world said I was supposed to have, I had. But I just got more depressed. I started to believe that something was missing. I began to think that maybe the emptiness had something to do with God.

I didn't even really think I believed in God. My spiritual exposure was limited to going to a group that met on Thursday nights at a nearby church. I'd drop in every so often because a pro surfer was leading it. I also thought some of the girls who went there were pretty cool, and there was always free pizza and stuff.

One night, I hit a low point. The feeling of emptiness overwhelmed me. I was totally depressed. I was lying on my bed when I looked over and saw the Bible that I had gotten at one of the Thursday night meetings.

I challenged God, "If you're real, just speak to me. I hear that this is supposed to be your word, and that your word never comes back empty. So if you're in it, show me."

I opened it up to Isaiah 1:18, which read, "'Come now, let us reason together,' says the Lord. 'Though your sins are like scarlet, they shall be as white as snow; though they are red as crimson, they shall be like wool.' If you are willing and obedient, you shall eat the best from the land, but if you resist and rebel, you'll be devoured by the sword."

That last part just stuck in my heart because I realized that I had been resisting and rebelling, partying, not really caring. Something inside clicked. Suddenly, a feeling came over me that was powerful and at the same time calming and peaceful. Although a lot of people had witnessed to me, it finally came down to just me and the Lord. I felt somehow as if God were in the room. It was then that I just gave myself to him.

The very next weekend, there was a surf contest in which pros and amateurs would be surfing against each other. One of my heroes, Scott Blake, would be there. I really wanted to try to beat him, even though I knew the chances of that were pretty slim.

When I paddled out to catch the first wave, it was an awesome, perfect wave. I felt like God's hand was on me somehow. After that first perfect wave came my way, I was pumped. I began to focus on the fact that God created the ocean, so he could make the good waves come to me if he wanted to. And then these perfect waves started coming. In a surfing contest where the surfers are pretty much on the same level, whoever gets the best waves is most likely to win. In every single round of the contest, the perfect wave would come to me—no one else but me. I'd get the best wave and win the heat. It never stopped.

The perfect waves kept coming my way until I ended up in the final round. I was thinking, *Lord, you're just going crazy!* Everyone was saying, "Bryan, I can't believe how well you're doing." I was like, "Yeah, uh, I became a Christian last week, and I don't know what's going on, but God's just blessing me, and waves are coming to me."

I ended up in the final, and sure enough, my hero was in it too, since he was the best surfer there. The same thing happened again—I got all the best waves. I also surfed my best and tried my hardest. With all of that combined, I ended up winning the contest!

At the age of 17, I had beaten my hero. All of my friends were like, "You just won—you just beat Scott Blake—I can't believe you did it!" Then they reminded me about a pro contest in Huntington Beach the very next day and kept pushing me to go. But I said, "That's crazy! There's no way."

But when I woke up the next morning, something inside told me to just go for it. So I drove up to Huntington Beach in time to enter the contest, and the same thing happened! Wave after wave after wave. I ended up in the semi-final. It was surreal.

While I was waiting around between heats, I met a team rep from Rip Curl wet suits. Half joking around and half serious, I said to him, "If I win this contest today, would you sponsor me?" He was like, "Sure, whatever. If you win it, I'll sponsor you."

I got back out there with a little more incentive. And I kept winning. The waves were coming to me exactly like the day before. God's hand was just on me. I couldn't even believe what I was seeing. It got to the point where I did-n't feel I deserved it; I didn't want it anymore.

So I paddled down the beach to an area where, due to a deep spot in the ocean, no waves had broken all day long. The other guys in my heat were way back down the beach, looking at me and probably thinking, *What is Bryan doing down there? He's crazy.*

I just sat on my board thinking about all my sins and the things that I had done wrong. It just reinforced how I didn't deserve to have God hand me this championship. I kept sitting there, talking to God saying stuff like, "Lord, I'm not going to let you bless me anymore. I'm just going to sit here where I know no waves are going to come."

As I was sitting there, out of the blue, a perfect wave came. At this point, I looked up to the heavens and half-shouted, "Lord, you are hilarious. I can't even believe this." So I took the wave, and sure enough, I ended up in the final round.

I surfed really well in the final, because, of course, God sent all the perfect waves my way. Close to the end of the heat, I began to resist the blessings God was giving me again. Then I felt God's voice say, "Get back out there and give it 110%. Do not quit. Just because I'm blessing you doesn't mean you can give up and not try your hardest."

I was thinking, *I'm tired; I've been surfing nonstop since yesterday. I'm not used to surfing this many times.* But I listened to what I thought God was saying to me and paddled back out with only two minutes remaining in the heat.

The second I got out there, a perfect wave came, and I caught it just as the horn blew to signal that the round was over.

As I waited for the judges to complete the scoring, I realized I would either get first place or second. Finally the head judge announced, "During the final seconds of the competition there was a tie, but because he caught the last wave in time, first place goes to Bryan Jennings."

At that moment, all of my dreams had come true. I'd officially become a professional surfer, I'd won prizes, and I'd gotten myself a sponsorship deal all in the same day. I was stoked beyond belief. The whole thing seemed totally unreal. My life had taken a dramatic turn.

I drove home with all this stuff in my car—they had given me one of those huge cardboard checks, which symbolized the money I was going to receive for winning. For the first time, I wouldn't have to get some lame summer job and could concentrate on surfing instead. I was freaking out, going from tears to screaming with joy.

Then suddenly I realized that there was no way I could have pulled this off by myself. It had been God, without a doubt. I actually began to get kind of mad. It didn't feel right to me. I felt like I had somehow cheated. So I asked God, "Why'd you do this for me?" It was then that I clearly heard these words in my head: "Because my kindness leads you to repentance."

I didn't know it then, but what I had heard was actually Scripture straight from the Bible. I did know that what I heard in my head wasn't how I talk—but still, my heart stopped when I came across the actual passage in the Bible. The words in his reply to me that day turned out to be Romans 2:4, which says, "Or do you show contempt for the riches of his kindness, tolerance and patience, not realizing that God's kindness leads you toward repentance?"

That is when I knew that God had claimed me for his own.

I flashed back to the moment when I'd first picked up the Bible from my desk and challenged him to show me that his word was real. He didn't hold a bat over my head and force me to change my life, or to stop doing the things that didn't please him, or to push me into following him. He used my love of surfing to show me, through the miracle of one perfect wave after another, that he wanted to bless me and love me. He gave me "the best of the land," even when I resisted.

How cool is that?

Bryan Jennings

Filled

Immediately he stood up in front of them, took what he had been lying on and went home praising God. Everyone was amazed and gave praise to God. They were filled with awe and said, "We have seen remarkable things today."
—Luke 5:25-26

One of the happiest times in my life was also one of the scariest. My life was going great and I was about to make one of the biggest moves in my life—marrying the girl I loved. I was recording and playing with a band, Nitro Praise, and all was well. I had no holes in my life, or so I thought.

Then on Halloween night, at a show we did for a youth group in Southern California, I got really sick. Before the show started, I was standing around watching one of the DJs when I had an attack. It was suddenly really hard for me to breathe. I started gasping for air and felt as if I were going to pass out.

This happened again and again over the next few weeks. The gasping for air turned into fainting spells. Then, just about every time I'd take the stage to perform with my band, I would throw up. I could hardly get through the second song when one of the other of the symptoms I'd been having would kick in. It didn't happen at any other time—just when I was in a situation when my adrenaline would be pumping.

Finally it got so bad that one day, at a recording session for one of our CDs, I suddenly threw up all over recording artist Crystal Lewis. At that moment, I knew I had to deal with the problem somehow.

My soon-to-be mother-in-law had the brilliant suggestion to go see a doctor. I had obviously been avoiding that, but now it was the only thing I could do.

The doctor ran a bunch of tests on me. I felt like a lab rat after about the fourth hour of being poked with needles and hooked up to machine after machine. I don't know what the worst part was: being poked, or waiting an entire week for the results.

Finally, my doctor called and asked if I could come in as soon as possible. That didn't sound too promising to me, so I stopped what I was doing and booked it to the hospital. There, the doctor sat me down, brought out a model of a heart, and began talking to me in some kind of medical-speak. He was throwing out terms that I had heard only in biology class, but I hadn't done too well in that subject, so I stopped him and asked him for an interpretation.

In layman's terms, I had a hole in between the two atriums of my heart. I had been born with this hole, but it did not close up when I was a baby like it was supposed to. I would have to have surgery as soon as possible.

My wedding was coming up, and all I could think was that my wife would end up a widow. But if I didn't have the surgery, she'd be more likely to lose me than if I did. So we scheduled the surgery for two months after the wedding. In the meantime, I had to make some changes, like getting a job that was less stressful, that wouldn't get me as hyped up as performing with the band did. It was really difficult to stop performing, especially since the band was doing really well and the guys depended on me.

I ended up getting a job at Starbucks. Oh yeah... there's nothing like injecting caffeine into a bad heart. Any time my heart beat faster, blood without oxygen would seep through the hole and go straight to my brain. Talk about being an airhead—that was me after a cup of coffee. I soon figured it out, and no matter how tempting the smell of coffee was every day at work, I stopped drinking it.

Time flew by and the day of my wedding came. I will never forget that day. My heart was beating so fast that I just knew that I was going to fall over before I said "I do," but it didn't turn out that way. When I saw my wife-to-be walking toward me, it was as if God touched my heart and said to me, "Here's my gift to you." And I gladly received it. Our honeymoon was great, and I treasured the days we spent together before the surgery.

The day of the surgery arrived, and as my wife and I sat there waiting for my number to be called, she leaned over and said, "Did they tell you what they're going to do?" I looked at her with fear in my eyes. She explained it even though she knew I was freaking out. "They start off by packing you in ice. Then they cut you open. They have to saw through your ribs and when they get to your heart, they stop it. You'll be on a machine that keeps you alive. The head surgeon will cut into your heart and fix the hole. Then he will sew you back up and get your heart started again."

At that point, I was thinking of running out of the hospital when a nurse came to get me. He had a "WWJD" chain around his neck. I asked him straight up, "Are you a Christian?" He looked at me and said, "Everything is going to be okay, Mr. Barbee."

As he was prepping me, we were talking about how awesome God is. My wife came in and prayed aloud, "Lord God, touch and heal my husband," just before they took me into the operating room. Then they shut the door behind her, and it crossed my mind that that might be the last time I would see her.

My nurse left the room and I was alone. Time was passing quickly, and I chattered on to God. "Lord, I know you are the creator, I know you are the King of kings and the Lord of lords, but I'm having a hard time believing that you're my healer. Have your way, Father, your will be done in me this day."

About that time, a man with dreadlocks came into the room humming. I thought to myself, *Please don't let him be my doctor.* He came over to me with a big needle and said, "Hey Mon, this will make you feel better." As he was giving me the injection, I asked him, "Are you a Christian?" He finished and laid down the needle. Then he began to sing the worship song, "Lord, I lift your name on high…"

It was amazing. I realized that I had been surrounded by Christians from the moment I walked into the hospital. I knew I was being supported and loved. My family had flown in from Texas to be there and was out in the waiting room, praying for me. My dad was praying that God would heal me. People I didn't even know were praying for me, through our following for the band, through churches...it was very cool.

The surgery began, and they placed a little camera inside my chest so that they could see my heart on a TV screen. My records were there, showing the location and size of the hole that had been there since birth. Now they were double-checking the situation to see if there had been any recent changes and to be certain about what they were dealing with. The "before picture" was on one screen. The doctors were studying that and comparing it to the live shot from the camera in my heart. There were eight surgeons all looking back and forth at what was on the screen and what was on my previous records.

I heard one of the doctors grunt, saying, "That's strange," and another one whispering. This continued for a few minutes.

My curiosity finally couldn't stand it anymore, and I was feeling kind of gutsy, so I asked the head surgeon, "Doctor, do you see Jesus in my heart?" He laughed and continued to work, and then he went over to the other doctors and they talked some more.

After their huddled consultation, the doctor walked over to me and said, "To answer your question, no, I didn't see Jesus, but I also did not find any evidence of a hole in your heart."

No trace of the hole was visible. No scar tissue remained to indicate it had closed up and healed itself. My heart was absolutely perfect. They sewed me up and cancelled the surgery.

I looked up at the surgeon again and told him, "If you don't see the hole, then you are seeing Jesus, because only his love and power are capable of filling the hole in my heart."

J.R. Barbee

Huge Twist of Fate

*Not to us, O Lord, not to us but to your name be the glory,
because of your love and faithfulness.*
—**Psalms 115:1**

One of the most amazing blessings God has given us came at a time when we thought he had abandoned us.

We had just released our CD, Underdog, and had finished a video for the song "Get Down," and everything had turned out great. Still, we felt that in order to complete the project, we needed to put together one more video. The problem was that we didn't have enough money left in our budget to make another one.

Then, out of nowhere, the youth ministry organization Teen Mania called us, saying that they loved our song from the CD called "Hands and Feet." They wanted to know if they could use it as a theme song in a video that would encourage teens to go on mission trips and serve people all over the world.

Of course we told them that we'd love to get behind that. It looked to us like God was blessing the Underdog project by paving the way for the other video we had hoped for, and he was intending to use it in a powerful way.

The chorus of "Hands and Feet" repeats this refrain; "I wanna be your hands, I wanna be your feet—I'll go where you send me, go where you send me." Well, God decided to send us to Panama to shoot the video. Within weeks, we were on our way to a place that was deep in the Darien Jungle with a group of leaders from Teen Mania and some teens participating in one of their mission trips.

Unfortunately for us, it quickly became more like a mission into pandemonium.

We had all kinds of trouble just getting there. Our flights were delayed, and we finally arrived at the Panama airport at about one in the morning. From there, we had to drive for another three hours, only to find that we had another journey ahead of us—this time on some boats that looked like logs with motors on the back. That part of the journey lasted six more hours. At this point, not having slept for an entire day, the trip seemed endless as we slowly made our way up the river crammed into these log-like boats.

So far, not good.

By the time we got to the village, we were about eight hours behind schedule. A successful video shoot usually takes about two days, and our shooting time had already been dramatically cut back. We began to doubt that God's hand was on this at all. The next news we received made it seem like God was playing a big joke on us.

The village chief decided not to allow us to shoot the video. We had just traveled all the way to Central America by plane, bus and sort-of boat, with no sleep, only to have the whole video shoot crash and burn before our exhausted eyes.

There wasn't much we could do at that point except try to get some rest, but that didn't go too well, either. Our "hotel" was basically just a few grass huts with dirt floors and mats on the dirt. There was no catering, no room service—nothing like that. Then we realized that these huts sat right next to the river, which was full of alligators. We were supposed to sleep on a ledge about 12 feet above the water, surrounded only by mosquito netting and alligators waiting for dinner.

We were thinking, *Okay, Lord. What have you gotten us into? We can't shoot any footage, we're hungry and tired, and now we're going to be alligator food?*

The next morning we woke up with big, nasty bites all over us—from mosquitoes, not alligators.

We still had no permission to shoot the video, so while we were waiting to be picked up, we killed time playing with the local village kids. Ben had some fun tossing them off the ledge into the river, and they loved every minute of that. They didn't seem to be intimidated by alligators—must be a local thing.

In the early afternoon, the chief unexpectedly showed up, and told us through a translator that he had suddenly changed his mind. We could film in his village after all.

We just sat there in a state of confusion, trying to figure out how to salvage the shoot in the little time we had left. We had to leave by four o'clock, so we only had about two hours to complete the whole video.

We began by shooting footage of the children while we played around in the water with them. The villagers started arriving in beautiful, colorful outfits. We shot some footage of them, and then we performed for about an hour at various spots around the village.

That was all we had time to do. We had to pack it in and make our way back up the river in the log-boats, and then we boarded a bus for another three-hour journey across the country just to get back to the airport.

On the way back, we had lots of time to talk. All of us felt that the trip had been a complete waste of time because the entire shoot was totally disorganized. We believed that the video would easily be the worst one we had ever made. On the boat ride back to Panama City, we were tempted to throw the footage into the water. It was that bad.

One thing was certain: we were definitely not trusting that God had been in control.

Three days after we got back, we got a call from the video director, urging us to come down and see the footage. He made it sound like it was going to be good. We thought, *Sure. Whatever. Let's go see it.* In our minds, there was no way we could have captured the emotion of the song in those couple of hours.

But when we got down to the studio and started viewing the footage, what we saw just blew us away. There before us were some of the most beautiful images we'd ever seen. It was like the hand of God was on every inch of footage.

We were stunned.

There were beautiful shots of kids from another culture learning about Jesus and people of all ages and from totally different backgrounds holding hands. But when we saw the footage of a villager who had leprosy having his hand touched by a teen from some place in middle America, it became undeniable to us that God *had* been on top of it the whole time.

When it was finished, it turned out to be the most compassionate, compelling, and emotional video that we'd ever made. We were very humbled to see how God had orchestrated this huge twist of fate to make such an amazing video. At the same time, he managed to reveal to us his great sense of humor.

That event shaped the way we look at our experiences now and what God can do with them. We learned to trust that he's got our backs, even when the alligators are snappin'.

Because of that video, thousands and thousands of teens have gone on Teen Mania mission trips around the world. Their lives have been changed, all as a result of those two days in the Darien Jungle. We, and many others, have been the hands and feet of God.

Audio Adrenaline

Gangster for God

Let the wicked forsake his way and the evil man his thoughts. Let him turn to the Lord, and he will have mercy on him, and to our God, for he will freely pardon.
—**Isaiah 55:7**

As I wiped away a young mother's tears, I recalled the anguish that I had seen in my grandmother's eyes and the tears she had for me.

These days I counsel gang members and their families. It hasn't always been that way; in my early years it was a much different story. My life was out of control, and I liked it that way.

I was born in Texas to an Apache Native American mother and a Chicano father. My father didn't even stick around to see what I looked like, and my mother died when I was three. Abandonment at that young age left me feeling worthless and scared. I didn't think that anybody loved me.

My great grandmother on my mother's side ended up taking me in. She gave me the name Dream-Bear after my Indian descent; I simply called her "Grandma." Her other grandchildren often got on her case for putting up with me, the troubled great grandson. She would tell them that God had put her here to love me as her own son. I was a frail, small boy who was scared to death. She became my wall, my protection.

By the age of 13, I was no longer frail: I was a well-known gang figure in South Texas and the type of person who could put a gun to your head in front of your mother. It wasn't unusual for me to come home at three in the morning covered in blood—mine and another person's. In her late 70s and half-paralyzed from a stroke, my grandma would get out of bed to warm up some dinner for me on her hotplate. When I was loaded on drugs, the demons in me would manifest themselves in terrible, violent outcries towards her. I would grab her, spit on her, push her down, pull her hair—you name it. Then I would suddenly realize what I was doing, fall to my knees, and put my head on her lap, and she would sing old spiritual songs in her native tongue. Her words would impact me in a way that I didn't understand.

When I was in jail, she would sit on the porch in her rocking chair and pray for me. She would ask God to make me a warrior of his kind.

When I was younger, she would send me to church to put a quarter in the offering plate, just to get me to go. When I returned, she would reward me with a dollar. She always told me there would be many churches and many preachers who would want me. She foresaw my future at a time when I couldn't even look at myself in the mirror. She loved me when even I didn't want to love me.

Eventually my life was so out of control that I cut off contact with her. I was ashamed and embarrassed to see her. I didn't want to overburden her. I figured that as soon as I got straight, I'd contact her, and she'd be proud of me.

I didn't know that it didn't matter to her—her unconditional love was there no matter what I did or whom I hurt, including her.

Years of gang-banging earned me the position of shot-caller. I was the one who would tell the other members who to kill or what to steal. One night two of my homeboys—Tommy and Armando—and I were partying in an old garage. We took some serious drugs and waited for them to kick in. We waited and waited and waited. But nothing happened.

Bored, I glanced at my watch. It was 2:05 in the morning.

When I looked back up, I noticed a brilliant light in the corner of the room. I asked my friends if they saw it. They said, "No, man, but we feel it." Then I heard a voice say my name. My name.

At that moment, I knew that it was the spirit of God that had come down upon us. I felt a kind of love filling my heart—a love that I had known before, but had never acknowledged. It was the kind of love that my grandma continued to show me all those years, unconditional and faithful.

I had always been dead set against believing in God. Besides, I thought that I had reached the point of no return. I'd think, *How in the world could God love someone who has done all the horrible things that I've done?* But the power of his love kept filling that old beat-up garage until it became bigger than the condemnation that I had placed on my soul. I felt forgiven, and I felt that he actually cared about me. Then I realized that if he could forgive me, of all people, then that would be reason enough for me to change.

I was delivered from my life of destruction that night. When I walked out into the night everything seemed different. The stars looked like huge diamonds, and the peace of God overwhelmed me. Suddenly I found myself quoting scripture to my friends. This was very odd, since the only time I had ever touched a Bible was to use the pages to roll a joint.

We found out later on that Tommy's aunt, a God-serving woman, had been awakened by the spirit of God at exactly two a.m. She clearly felt that he was asking her to pray for Tommy and his friends. Five minutes later, God made a house call, and our lives changed.

After that night, I never looked back.

Unfortunately that wasn't the case with Tommy and Armando. Two years later, Tommy died of an overdose, and Armando was killed in a gang-related incident.

Of all the people in my life back then, I'm the only one that's still here. I'm the one who toyed with the big rigs, the one who dared them to hit me; but God has kept me here in spite of my earlier life choices. Tommy and Armando felt the love in that garage that night, but they just couldn't hold onto it. I was able to latch on because I recognized it. My grandma showed me the same kind of love—love that doesn't make sense, the kind that sticks with you even when you don't deserve it and can't begin to understand it.

Soon after that night, I found out that my grandma had died from a heart attack. Her death was the hardest thing for me to deal with. I finally understood the love she had for me, but I never got to tell her that I loved her too, and that I was sorry. I never got to tell her I was saved. I never got to tell her that she was my hero.

Today I walk with the forgiveness I've been given. I know my grandma sees my life and looks down on me with a smile. I know in my heart and mind that her spirit lives in me. I've learned about the reality of forgiveness. I've learned that forgiveness is power. I don't need gangs and drugs in my life—I have Christ.

In the two years I've been working with gangsters, 17 of them have gotten out of gangs. That's 17 lives that God has helped me to save. Does it make up for the lives that I've helped to destroy? I don't know.

When I look into the eyes of the lost souls that I am determined to help, I tell them that the world is full of gangs. People need to feel like they belong. It isn't the gang that's the problem, it's what the people in it stand for, what actions they take, and what they get involved in that matters.

I'm still a gang member. But like Grandma always wanted, I'm a warrior of God's kind, a gangster for God. I'm in for life and the life hereafter.

See ya then, Grandma.

Roger Alejos Dream-Bear

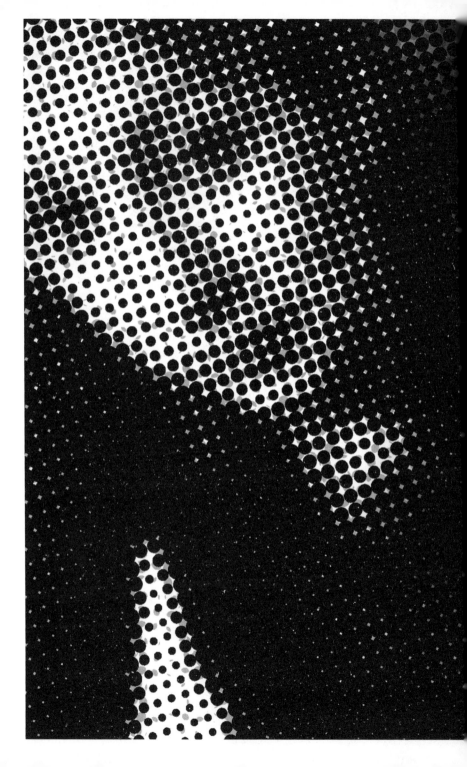

04

He is a God of
Mercy and Forgiveness

"Who is a God like you, who pardons sin and forgives the transgression of the remnant of his inheritance? You do not stay angry forever but delight to show mercy."
—**Micah 7:18**

"The Lord our God is merciful and forgiving, even though we have rebelled against him..."
—**Daniel 9:9**

"You are forgiving and good, O Lord, abounding in love to all who call to you."
—**Psalms 86:5**

From the Door of Death

I love the Lord, for he heard my voice; he heard my cry for mercy.
—Psalms 116:1

Have you ever been so addicted to lies that you don't recognize the truth?

Or have you ever been so afraid of love that you begin to starve yourself or purge yourself, just to get rid of the "you" inside?

I know how it feels to hate myself. And I know how it feels to be afraid of my own mind. I have felt that aching fear that holds a gun to my side. And I have let the voices in my head run my life.

Anorexia Nervosa controlled me for six years. During that period, I was hospitalized, went through every type of counseling, and experienced every kind of group therapy that exists. When you think about it, I really shouldn't even be here. There were many times that I was told my bones were going to break—right within my body. I had EKGs every day because my heart was down to beating 34 beats a minute when a healthy person's heart beats 60 to 80 beats a minute. I developed an arrhythmia that made my heart beat irregularly.

I was, quite simply, a mess.

At times I would get better, then I'd relapse, get better, then relapse. I was scared and couldn't understand why it wouldn't just go away. I believed that there was no hope, that no one could help me, that there was no way I would ever be free of the controlling thoughts. I remember thinking to myself, *Why can't I just choose to do the right thing?*

I spent much of high school in a psychiatric hospital. The hospital became my safe place—my home. I felt free in there—free from the cares and worries of the outside world. I didn't have to deal with the pressures of high school or the verbal abuse from my stepdad, who constantly told me that I had no common sense and demanded that I come straight home from school and go to my room.

For years, my stepdad took the anger he had towards my mom out on me. I was always in the middle—the pawn. He was over-controlling, and it seemed like I was always grounded. He controlled me in every way until I began to find control in how I ate—or didn't eat. It was my dysfunctional tool to cope with my feelings.

Although most of my friends were able to go out at night, my stepdad would never allow me to stay out after eight. As crazy as it sounds, I had to sneak out to go to Bible study. I had first accepted Christ when I was in ninth grade, but my parents wouldn't allow me to go to youth group because it was on a school night and didn't end until after 8 p.m.

With things the way they were in my family, I was hungry for true love and acceptance, and I found it through the people in the youth group. But after awhile, sneaking out got too difficult and led to too much drama, so I started focusing on other ways to gain some control and consistency. My faith kind of fell to the wayside.

Hopelessness took its place.

Growing up, no one in my family ever expressed feelings. Every time I felt an intense emotion, I felt bad and ashamed. I actually thought I was abnormal for having feelings, and I began to fear them.

My mom's family didn't know how to confront problems or communicate with each other, so we just didn't talk about certain things—like my real dad. I was just two when my mom left him. No one told me he existed until I was 13. By then, I had missed years of potential communication with him. The truth was swept under the rug when he and my mom parted ways, and my stepdad had raised me as his own.

Because of the loss of my real father, I became afraid of being abandoned again. So I made a decision to abandon myself first before I'd ever have to experience the pain of someone else leaving again.

I began using food as a way to express my anger, my fears, and even myself. Food was the one thing that no one could touch—that only I could control. I didn't choose to become anorexic overnight; rather, food became the method I used to deal with my feelings. I wound up in the hospital again and again.

The hospital gave me a vacation from myself, an escape from having to face my emotions. Up until this point, no one had dealt with my eating disorder as more than just an issue about eating. I had assumed that victory over an eating disorder would come when I was eating again, the weight was back on, and things were back to normal. I have learned through experience that freedom from an eating disorder is much more than that.

After I left the hospital the first time I immediately relapsed. I didn't know how to face reality again. I didn't know how to cope with my problems without the protection of starving and exercising. I dealt with my anger and fear through food. With that cycle still in place, I was back in the hospital again in no time.

Things were pretty boring day in and day out in the hospital. When I learned that I could attend a special church service held there, I figured that going would give me something to do. I had so much free time that I thought this would help me to fill it. I didn't think of going to the service in the same way as going to the youth group I had once loved. I figured it would be nothing like that. It wasn't, but it was.

There were no old friends, no cool youth pastor, and no activities that teens had fun doing. But it brought back the feeling of belonging and being accepted and loved, like the youth group had given me.

When I told my mom that I had gone to the service, I asked her if she would bring me my Bible. My life was so dark and awful that the comfort that I got from reading it became the only thing to hold onto. It was as if a light went on—like *Duh! How could I have forgotten about God?*

I was released from that hospital stay once I'd gained 30 pounds. I was expected to gain at least 10 more pounds at home. My mom, realizing that I might freak out when I saw myself for the first time in months (there were no mirrors in the hospital), had to put sheets over the mirrors. I was still pretty unstable, and the underlying reasons for my sickness hadn't been addressed. Being thrown back into the dysfunction of my family didn't help.

While I was gone, my parents had decided to get a divorce. When I got home, we had dinner together for the last time so that my parents could announce their plans. The night turned into a disaster. My stepdad stood up at the dinner table and screamed at me about how I had caused all the problems. He basically blamed me for the whole divorce—not exactly what I needed to hear at the time, and also not true. I just thought to myself, *What's new?*

Life at my house was a mess. I quickly discovered that my mom was dealing with her own issues, with the divorce and the demands on her from the business she owned. I took on the mother role around the house—picking up my brother and sister, making their lunches. Mom just couldn't figure out how to relate to me in addition to dealing with her own problems. She got so overwhelmed that she began to avoid going to work and started looking for ways to cope—or not—with all that was going on. She basically wasn't around, and I was left to hold it together for my siblings and myself.

At this point I had been through every group and every kind of treatment that I knew of. None of it had cured me from my illness. Now, with all of these new stressors, I knew that if I continued in this downward spiral and kept depriving my body of the nutrients that it needed to survive and stay healthy, the damage could be permanent, even fatal.

One night I was sitting on the sofa crying. I was angry with God because I was so miserable. I decided to put it all out on the table and be really honest. So I told him that I didn't trust him and that I didn't know if he really loved me. How could I tell other people that God loved them if I didn't know his love myself? I told him desperately that I was not going to get off the sofa until he somehow showed himself to me. I had no idea what to look for. I knew that things weren't going to start falling from heaven or anything. Eventually, I went off to bed.

But things slowly began to change.

The only thing I can compare it to is driving by a building every day noticing construction workers on the site. A few weeks later, there's a foundation and framing. Six months later, there's a huge, beautiful new structure there. You're amazed at the finished product, but you didn't really notice all the work that was put into it.

In the same way, a work was being done in me, through the way I handled my food. I was able to sit down and have a meal and enjoy it—and I was able to know that I was hungry or full. My bones began to heal, and I started feeling stronger. Things began to heal between my family and me. I slowly changed the way that I viewed myself and others, and I developed a new way of handling confrontations and situations.

The change came over months, but as I looked back, I could see the evidence of my release from the issues I had struggled with for years. Everything began to smooth out. God's fingerprints were all over the whole thing, because there was no way that I could have done it on my own. I had not been able to function in a healthy way for years.

The peace and sense of security that I experienced through him was enormous. And once I began to trust God with my life, the urge to starve myself in order to be in control of things began to fade. It was the most freeing thing that I have ever experienced.

I slowly learned to grieve through the pent-up emotions that I had buried throughout my life. I began to have hope that I would come out of my anorexia alive, as opposed to being one of those statistics that don't make it. And believe me, many of the seven million people that suffer from an eating disorder in the United States don't.

People with eating disorders know that achieving victory is a long, hard road that few are willing to take. It means going against the standards of our society and opinions of others. It means being willing to be open and vulnerable.

The grip of anorexia held me completely captive for years. Nothing but God changed the way it controlled my life.

I am not saying that I am never tempted anymore, or that I don't think about food, but with the power of God in my life, I am able to face each challenge and walk through it in freedom. God has given me the strength to keep from going back to my old ways of coping.

When I thought I couldn't hold on anymore, he held me up and helped me get through the darkest of times. And he has continued to show himself to me ever since.

He is always there when I need him.

Some became fools in their rebellious ways and suffered afflictions because of their iniquities. They loathed all food and drew near the gates of death. Then they cried to the Lord in their trouble, and he saved them from their distress. He sent forth his word and healed them; he rescued them from the grave. Let them give thanks to the Lord for his unfailing love and his wonderful deeds for men. Let them sacrifice thank offerings and tell of his works with songs of joy.
—Psalms 107:17-22.

Katherine Blake

Accountability

But encourage one another daily, as long as it is called Today, so that none of you may be hardened by sin's deceitfulness.
—**Hebrews 3:13**

I couldn't process all the thoughts that were going through my head. I was standing in the hallway of my apartment, holding in my hands an object that would change my life forever. The pink line on the pregnancy test was something I hadn't thought I would see for a long time. I was only 18 years old. My heart was in my stomach. My first reaction was "How can I hide this? What brought me to this point?"

At the age of two, I started mimicking my mother's singing, as she would practice her music in our living room. I remember being seven years old, when the sounds of worship would find their way into my upstairs bedroom. I would stay awake to listen to her voice singing into the night. My whole family had musical talent—that is where my love for music began.

At the age of 13, I entered a singing contest in Irvine, California, and won a cruise. My only purpose for entering the contest was to win the cruise and have fun. I didn't think that I would be approached by a record label executive and asked to sign a record deal, but that's what happened, and I stayed with that company for several years.

When I was 15, I signed with another label, and everything took off from there. My schedule became very crazy. I had to be homeschooled in order to keep up with all my travel arrangements; I was flying back and forth between California and Nashville, Tennessee, recording an album.

The record was released in 1998, and life became even crazier. I was always on the road, always away from my parents. I began to lose the close accountability in my life that I once had. My concerts were often scheduled on Sundays, so I missed a lot of church. In ministry, you have to be filled in order to give out—and my well was running dry.

I began to feel a loneliness on the road that I had never felt before. It was an emptiness that I didn't know how to handle. At the age of 17, I had never had a boyfriend and certainly never any sexual contact with a male. It was something I was proud of.

One day I met a guy, Ryan. He was one of the first guys to ever give me his phone number, and I was pretty excited. We began to talk on the phone a lot. We both traveled quite a bit—Ryan was in a Christian rock band—and we had a lot of phone conversations, which resulted in some very expensive cell phone bills. Occasionally we would see each other on the road if we happened to be in the same city.

Ryan's attention started to make me feel good about myself. He seemed to relieve a lot of the loneliness I felt, to fill a void in my life. I didn't realize then that this emptiness could only be filled by the love of God.

After awhile we decided to start "courting." We both had read dating books and liked the idea of courting. We didn't want to date for the sake of dating. Rather, we wanted to court with the intention of marriage. We started our relationship with some strict guidelines for ourselves about our physical interaction. But we lacked something that later would prove crucial—outside accountability.

I often spoke of abstinence in my concerts. I always told teenagers to have guidelines for themselves in dating relationships. I thought I would always be strong in any situation.

Ryan and I became engaged. It was late summer of 1999, and we set a wedding date of June 11, 2000.

I turned 18 that summer. I packed up my belongings from my family's house in California and moved to Nashville, where Ryan was.

Ryan and I found ourselves changing the physical guidelines we had set for ourselves, bit by bit. It seemed easy. After all, we were going to be married in a few months. Making out wasn't a big deal, right?

What we didn't realize was how difficult it would be to stop once we started.

And soon I found myself asking the question "Could I be pregnant?" I found myself in the bathroom, staring at a pregnancy test. I really didn't think I could be, but I needed to take it.

So I took the test... and my worst fears became reality. It was positive. Tears flooded my face. I didn't like myself or what I had done. I had lost something that I'd always held so precious in my life—my innocence.

I ran into the other room to tell Ryan. The reality of it all really didn't sink in. I had gotten a shot for a sore throat earlier that day, and I thought that it might have made the test come out positive. So I bought three more tests, but they all came out the same way. I still didn't believe it, so we rushed over to a walk-in clinic. Their test came out positive. I asked a nurse in the office if the shot could alter the results, and she said no. My heart dropped and I started to cry uncontrollably. How could this be?

My first thought was, *How can I hide this?* Suddenly I realized that everyone was going to know what I had done: my parents... my record company... my management... my booking agency... my friends... my fans... GOD.

The thought of getting married right away and telling people it was a honeymoon baby passed through my mind. I couldn't do that. Other thoughts went through my mind, but only one gave me peace. We decided to get married and get off the road.

Within a few weeks I was married, pregnant, in Nashville, away from my family, and off the road. I felt extremely alone. On top of that, I was very sick throughout my entire pregnancy; I was in bed for the first five months. Sitting in bed alone, I had a lot of time to think. I was depressed. I was ashamed. I felt unworthy to pray.

I thought I had gone so far that God's hand would not reach me.

But God continually spoke to my heart about his forgiveness and restoration: that it applied to my life, and that no matter how far away I went, his love goes much further.

I began to pray again. One day I came to the full realization that Jesus died and carried my guilt so that I wouldn't have to carry it. That was the day that I let go and put control of my life back in the hands of God. How amazed I was that I could start over.

My guilt was lifted and I focused upon the blessings of my life. In spite of my stupidity, God decided to bless me with a beautiful daughter, Jaslyn Taylee. I thank God for her daily.

I made some bad choices, and I will never condone the actions that led to my pregnancy. I can say that I have learned and grown a lot. When I found out that I was pregnant, Ryan and I realized that we needed to get some spiritual accountability in our lives, so we quickly sought out some wonderful pastors and others with whom we could share our lives. Their encouragement, wisdom, and advice were an enormous gift to us.

God has given me a ministry speaking to young teenage girls. I encourage them, assuring them that even though they may have made bad choices in their lives, it doesn't mean they can't turn it around and make it right. We are all worth so much to God.

More than anything, I encourage everyone to find someone in whom they can confide. Talk things through—decisions, temptations, and even dreams. It's amazing how much better life can be when we walk through it alongside each other.

Nikki Leonti

The Family Across The Way

This is what the Lord Almighty says: "Administer true justice; show mercy and compassion to one another."
—**Zechariah 7:9**

When I was just starting life out on my own, my first apartment was in a cheap complex full of college kids and young working roommates. The one exception was a family who lived across from me in an apartment not much bigger than my one-bedroom place. My window faced their window, and neither of us had drapes.

I was busy waiting tables at night and taking classes at the local community college during the day. My family was more than a little upset that I had dropped out of the state university, and I was still feeling guilty about wasting their money. We weren't exactly burning up the phone lines between us.

I did a lot of vicarious living through the family across the way. They were like a modern version of the Waltons. Really.

The kid would sit at the kitchen table drinking a glass of milk with a plate of dollar store cookies beside him, coloring pictures. The mom ran around with some sewing she took in, and around five o'clock each evening the dad came in and tossed his thin jacket on the flimsy coat rack. Mother and son jumped up from whatever they were doing and hugged him as if he'd been gone for a week. I swear.

If I hadn't seen it with my own eyes, I wouldn't have believed it either.

The week before Christmas, I made a quick trip home to visit my family. As a new waiter, I was scheduled to work straight through the holidays, so I had to make it short. We opened a few gifts, hugged a lot, and after two days I was right back in my apartment.

A few days later, I was watching the family across the way, as usual, and I noticed that things looked different. The kid was at the table, but there was no glass of milk. No plate of cookies. The mom was sewing, but she could hardly hold her head up. Five o' clock came. Five o' clock went. No dad. No jacket on the coat rack. I waited, holding off my evening restaurant shift until the very last minute. By 5:50 there was still no sign of the dad.

I checked their front door on my way to work, hoping against hope that my fears were unfounded. But there, large and round on their solemn front door, hung a funeral wreath. It was still fresh.

I cried on the way to work, as if the man had been my own father. I thought about their cheap apartment and cramped living space and wondered how they would ever manage without him. Memories of their smiles and laughter went through my head all night, and I don't know how I ever made it through my shift.

On the way home, I thought about what I could do to help. I knew that it was still too soon to offer condolences. And who was I to them, anyway? What would they think if some college punk in a skinny goatee and a tip apron knocked on their door and admitted that he'd been a peeping Tom for the last six months?

Days went by and the family across the way grew more pitiful by the hour. They sat. They stood. They came in and out of focus. Their grief could be felt all the way to my side of our green and tan building. Carols chimed over the radio, and garish red and green cartoons splashed across the TV, yet nothing changed. For the first time in my life I realized what was meant by the term "holiday blues."

That's it! I thought as I threw on my uniform for my Christmas Eve shift. The family across the way hadn't hung a single string of tinsel or bough of holly. I didn't think they'd even turned on a single light since the man of the house had passed away. *Maybe a Christmas tree would help cheer them up.*

I bustled through work, overflowing with false holiday cheer and pushing my good graces to the limit all night so that my tables would be generous with holiday tips. It worked, and I sped off after my shift to scout for late-night tree lots.

Unfortunately, such things only exist in cheesy holiday specials on TV. All of the tree stands were closed and the 24-hour mega-stores were even out of the fake kind. I cursed myself for waiting until the last minute to do something nice for those two lost souls across the way. Still upset, I pulled into a gas station on the way home. The least I could do was to bring them a care package of milk and Christmas cookies for the little kid.

The wizened old lady behind the counter sucked on a cigarette and watched carefully as I loaded a little red basket with cold cuts and orange juice, candy canes and eggnog. As I made my way up to the counter I spotted a tabletop tree beside the cash register.

"Is your tree for sale?" I asked around her halo of cigarette smoke.

"It is now," she croaked when she saw the stack of ones and fives in my eager hand. "30 bucks," she said without flinching.

"30 bucks?" I said. "But... it's Christmas Eve!"

"I know," she said, smiling. "You should have heard what I charged the last guy. You're getting a deal."

I bundled up the tree in one of her plastic sacks and brought it to my place to air it out a little before I brought it to the family across the way. I stacked a plate with cold cuts and cheese and another with cookies and chocolates, and then covered them in plastic wrap. I plugged the tree in to test the lights and burn off a little of the nicotine smell from the old lady's ever-present cigarettes.

Then, just for a second, I sat down in my dilapidated, second-hand easy chair to see how it would look to the family across the way.

A knock at the door woke me much later. I sprang to my feet, spying the warm plates of food and brightly blazing tree still sitting on my small dinner table. How long had I been asleep?

I opened the door to find the mother and son from across the way. Their faces looked concerned and they pointed to the tree.

"We saw the tree lights still burning and you sleeping beside it," they said shyly. "We were worried that you would burn your apartment down."

I saw the little boy eyeing the chocolate and cookies so I quickly invited them in. I sat them down and found a station playing carols on the radio while they ate. I poured eggnog and orange juice and sat down quietly beside them.

I sneaked a peek out of my window at their dark and dismal apartment. How bright and alive my tree must have seemed to them as they whiled away the lonely hours of their first Christmas Eve without the man of the house. And how pitiful I must have looked beside the tree, sitting there in my broken down chair, all alone on Christmas. How incredible that in the depths of their despair, they could still feel sorry for me.

I had been so eager to surprise them. To rush home and get everything ready. To knock on their door and show them that the world was not such a horrible place.

To offer them a miracle.

But in the end, the little family from across the way had brought the miracle to me.

Rusty Fischer

My Secret Life

"Watch and pray so that you will not fall into temptation. The spirit is willing, but the body is weak."
—Matthew 26:41

I lay in my bed and stared up into the darkness. Nervously, I was praying, "Lord, I need your help. I can't do this alone. Please, please, Lord Jesus, help me."

I stopped praying and started thinking. My thoughts drifted back toward my past as I began to fall asleep.

I thought about how I was 16 years old and a slave to pornography. Sadly, I recalled the three years of behaviors that had led up to this point. At first, I was just into looking at clothing catalogs. Then I progressed to watching movies like Striptease and Disclosure. Thoughts of some of the foreign films I'd seen sickened me. I felt like I was hopelessly lost in sin.

Then I thought about where I was—at church camp. I was a junior counselor.

Somehow I had gotten to be a church camp employee without having to admit my problem with pornography. Nobody knew about my secret life except God and me.

I turned my mind toward happier thoughts. This had been a wonderful week. I'd been able to get away from my addiction and felt closer to God than I had ever been. The fellowship with the kids in my group and the other counselors was great. The spiritual atmosphere and intensity was something I hoped would never go away as long as I lived. I didn't even want to think about pornography, much less return to looking at it.

But then I thought about that night's campfire. The theme of the night had been how sin can hurt your relationship with God. The camp director, David, had demonstrated this fact by throwing water on the campfire until it went out. In the pitch-black darkness he said, "When I put out the fire, it was like when we sin. We drown out the light of God in our lives." But then he took some hay and matches and relit the fire. It took a long time to light, because the wood was wet. He went on to say, "It was hard to get the fire back because there was so much water present. It's the same in our lives. It's hard for God's light to return once we've put it out with sin."

I could relate to everything he said that night. At the end of the campfire, the topic of pornography and hidden sin was brought up. I listened intently as David briefly explained the dangers of pornography.

Then, out of the blue, the camp director asked me and another counselor to come up and pray for anyone who might be struggling with hidden sin. I walked up to the campfire with the other counselor. He prayed first, and then I did. I prayed, "Dear Lord Jesus, I pray for those here who are struggling with sin. I know you've said that if we confess our sin then you will forgive us. So I pray that those struggling would confess to you and ask for forgiveness and help to repent, because without your help we can't do anything. I also pray that they would ask for help from others to keep them accountable. Amen."

As I prayed, a knot grew steadily in my throat. I had been praying for myself as much as anyone in the group around the campfire. That campfire had been the most moving thing that I had ever experienced.

Walking away, I thought about my testimony that I had to give in the morning. Before the campfire, I had planned to talk about how I became a Christian, but now I knew what I had to do. I was going to tell the truth.

When I got back to the cabin, I took the notes I had made for my testimony and tore them up. I had known when I had written those notes that what I prepared was not what God wanted me to say. I had tried to ignore God's urgings to tell the truth.

My thoughts now drifted back to the present. What was I going to say tomorrow? I had no idea. Again I prayed, "Dear Lord, please give me the words to say and the guts to say them. Amen."

My eyes flickered shut and I fell asleep.

I awoke the next morning with butterflies in my stomach. As I ate breakfast and had devotions with my group, my stomach continued to flutter more and more. Nervously, my heart started jumping around in my chest, and my palms started to sweat. By the time morning worship came around, I was more nervous than I had been in years.

As each song was sung, I knew the time for my testimony was closer. I still had no idea what I was going to say. All I knew was that I was trusting in God. I wasn't going to question what he wanted me to do.

Finally, the time for my testimony came. Somehow my legs carried me up to the front. My whole body felt shaky with nervousness. I opened my mouth and prayed that God would give me the words to say.

"Hi," I shakily began. "When I first decided to do my testimony, I don't know why I chose this morning. But I think I know now. I'd planned to tell you about how I became a Christian at an early age because of my fear of hell. But last night's campfire changed all that. Instead, I'm going to tell you the truth about my life, and that is that I've fallen away from God."

I paused to take a breath. There was complete silence in the room. 100 faces that I had only just begun to know stared back at me.

"For a long time, I've been doing things that I know are wrong. I've been looking for light in darkness. But this week has changed my life. Uh, and that's all. Thanks."

I hardly knew what I'd said. I didn't know where the words I chose even came from, but since this was a kids' camp with first to sixth graders involved, I didn't want to blow them away with the specifics of what I was dealing with. Still, I never could have given that testimony without God giving me the words and the courage to say them. I found that God can do anything if I just listen and obey.

I had finally taken the first step toward coming clean with the fact that I was living a secret life. I could sense that this was a turning point for me.

I started back to my seat amid the customary clapping that had followed every testimony that week. But then one of the counselors stood up and suggested that they pray for me. So I went back up, and the two camp directors and my senior counselor prayed for me. I felt like jelly as I stood there receiving their prayers.

When they finished, I got hugs from five counselors. I was surprised that I didn't mind, because I'm not a hugging kind of a guy. I felt wonderful. I felt like God could change my life.

Then the counselors asked if there was something specific that I would like to talk to them about, but I told them that I wanted to talk to my parents first. I am very close to them, and they are the kind of people I could feel safe telling just about anything. I knew that they would listen to me and show that they really cared about what I was going through, no matter what it was.

After I got home I shared with my parents what I had been struggling with. It felt good to finally get it out in the open.

Although I wish I could say that my struggles are over, I still have a problem avoiding pornographic materials. I guess that my human weakness is something that I'll have to continue giving over to God through prayer, and that's what I am doing.

But after God worked in my life like he did at camp, for the first time I realized that he really can do anything.

I'm holding on to that.

Daniel J. Hill, 17

Grateful in Michigan

He has showed you, O man, what is good. And what does the Lord require of you? To act justly and to love mercy and to walk humbly with your God.
—Micah 6:8

It was the week of Thanksgiving: the prelude to the hustle and bustle of the Christmas season. Two months after the World Trade Center had been taken down by terrorists and thousands of people had lost their lives—hundreds of kids had lost one or both parents—I was disturbed by the comments that I was hearing from my peers at school.

"I don't have anything to be thankful for," I heard one of them smugly announce during a discussion in English class. *What?* my mind screamed. My stomach dropped as I thought of the elderly Haitians who were grateful for the shoes I had given them and the babies who were temporarily pulled from their misery as I picked them up to comfort them.

I had just returned from a trip to Haiti where I learned what it meant to step out of my comfort zone. It was as if I were living in a page from National Geographic, and all the smells, sights, and people of that region came alive to me.

Not a moment was spent in comfort as I assisted the medical team that went to help the Haitians that live daily without the luxuries that we take for granted: indoor plumbing and paved roads, electricity and air conditioning. Devoid of such things, the people we encountered rarely had the opportunity to bathe. The resulting smell was nearly impossible to tolerate. I found myself holding my breath often as I knelt down to help fit shoes on barefoot elderly Haitians. As I presented the simple things I had to offer—clothes, toys, shoes, and laughter—their gracious smiles never failed to remind me of our similarities. Our human needs were the same. It was just that mine were met most of the time, and theirs weren't.

I saw many heartbreaking ailments, but nothing touched me more that week than the short half-hour visit we made to Mother Teresa's Home for Sick and Malnourished Babies on our last day there. I was the only student who ended up going along with the six adults from our group.

We pulled up to the gate and got out of the van as a nun approached to let us in. Behind the nun, a small girl was shouting, "Hello!" greeting us excitedly. A closer look at her revealed the poor condition of this cheerful little girl. Her ear was encircled with dried blood, and the sides of her mouth were encrusted with scabs. I shifted nervously as I followed the nun, wondering if all the children would look so unhealthy. The girl scurried off when we entered the building.

Even before we saw any children, we could hear them. The whining sound of kids crying tends to annoy me, so the sound of a few dozen wailing babies was nearly unbearable. The heat in the room was suffocating, and I watched beads of sweat drip down the noses of some of the adults. I held my breath as I entered the first room, preparing for what I might see or smell.

The sight was heart-wrenching. The room was lined with the cribs of tiny crying infants. The rows of sick babies seemed to go on forever. Their mattresses were stained from accidents and broken down from old age.

At first, I was paralyzed with helplessness. Some of the others in my group began smiling and talking to the babies, so I quickly followed their example.

The adjacent room was for the children with tuberculosis. When we entered the room, I became embarrassed at my hesitation to play with them. I was worried about the possibility of catching the disease, but I suppressed my concerns and showered them with as much attention as I could muster.

Suddenly, the sound of tiny voices singing could be heard coming from another part of the building. I followed the group in the direction of the music. In the dining room, two dozen older, healthier toddlers, having just finished their meal, were welcoming us with a special song. *"De rien, tra la la, merci merci vous!"* they sang. The French translated to "Welcome and thank you!"

I choked back tears as these attention-starved children hurried toward us. It was simply impossible for the handful of nuns to give the nearly 100 children living there individual attention each day. Desperate to be held and hugged, the kids tugged at our clothes.

A short time passed, and one of the nuns called the children back to another room. We turned to leave, and the kids cried out to us as we did our best to give them last-minute hugs and smiles. As I was turning toward the exit, I spotted a baby girl in a tiny rocking chair holding her arms out as she cried. I went over and picked her up, and she instantly stopped crying. She rested her head on my shoulder, and I spoke softly to her, more to soothe myself than to comfort her. The hard bloat of her belly pressed against my own full stomach as I rocked her back and forth. Her feeble legs crumpled under her and I found it difficult to cradle her delicate frame.

Overcome with hopelessness, I thought of all the children who would never leave that building. I felt selfish and spoiled as I thought of the country and the life to which I would return the next day. I realized what a gift from God it was to have been born in the US, into the family I belonged to: to have the luxury of living in a country that offers everyone equal opportunity and is stable and well-developed. Simply being born in America, even without the best family or economic situation, is still a hundred times better than living in the environment and economic situation that we observed that week.

I handed the head nun a fistful of money as I left in a pitiful attempt to calm my own conscience. God had shown such mercy to me by giving me the life I had that I wanted—needed—to try to give anything and everything I could to these poor, miserable little ones in return.

Now, a month before Christmas, I sat in the classroom full of students who had been sheltered from the realities of how so many people live in other parts of the world. *If only they could know how much we have and how much we take for granted,* I thought. *Maybe they'd be more grateful.*

I shook my head sadly for a moment, and then something inside of me welled up and I found myself raising my hand.

"I'd like to tell the class about my visit to Haiti," I began.

Elizabeth A. Glover, 17

Owning Up

He who conceals his sins does not prosper, but who-ever confesses and renounces them finds mercy. Blessed is the man who always fears the Lord, but he who hardens his heart falls into trouble.
—Proverbs 28:13-14

Once in a while things get a little blurry. It's like: you start out with your eyes focused on God, but you slowly stray away, experience trials—and then you come back to God, and he's right where you left him.

After years of being in bands that played only secular music and feeling burdened that what we were playing didn't have much to do with our faith, some friends and I started a band called Slick Shoes. It wasn't intended to be a full-blown ministry band, but at least we'd be able to share that we were Christians and use our talents to glorify God.

A couple of years down the road, as we got more popular, we kind of lost sight of that. We were a little selfish with the notoriety we had gained and were caring more about how cool we were rather than remembering why we do what we do in the first place. That's when we hit our lowest point ever and began to deal with a whole lot of trials.

We were on the road touring, but nothing was going right. We were spending more money than we were earning. Even though we had a brand new van, it repeatedly broke down. There were times when we'd fill it with gas while it was still running, because if we shut it off, we wouldn't be able to get it started again.

Sometimes we'd be stuck at gas stations for hours waiting for help when our van wouldn't start. People saw dollar signs when we walked in, and we'd get overcharged for repairs because we were helpless and at the mercy of the folks who had what we needed.

Things got so bad that sometimes we ended up in a seedy dive that was a rent-by-the-hour hotel, because when we'd get stranded in some not-on-the-tour town, it would be the only place we could afford. That was often worse than trying to sleep in the van, because at like four in the morning, strangers would come banging on the door looking for someone else. It was pretty hectic.

When it got to the point where we were completely broke, we'd have to call our parents to wire us money. We finally began staying the night in the homes of complete strangers, because we couldn't even afford rent-by-the-hour dives.

The worst part, though, was getting calls from my wife wondering where we were going to get the money to pay our bills. I battled with that a lot. Although we had all felt called to do this, we began to question how this could be what God wanted us to be doing if we were jeopardizing our families and not making enough to even support ourselves on the road.

Finally, we ended up in Texas at someone's house whose mom said we could stay the night. While we were there, I was scheduled to do a phone interview with a magazine. Suddenly, in the middle of our conversation, the reason we might be going through all these hardships just struck me.

When I hung up the phone, I got down on my knees and surrendered everything to God right then and there. I admitted to him that we'd been taking more of the credit than we'd been giving to him and doing everything our own way without involving him. I even confessed that I had lost sight of the fact that I could play drums because he had blessed me with a gift.

Then I asked him with an open heart if this was really what he wanted us to be doing. I was honestly ready to give it all up if I knew for sure that I was not doing what he wanted. If it meant that I worked at Pizza Hut or as a janitor in a jail for the rest of my life, at least I would know that I was doing his will and that his blessing was on it. I was no longer sure of his will, because I'd been ignoring God and trying to do everything in my own strength.

Not long after I surrendered everything to him in that prayer, his answer became clear. The van stopped breaking down, and our bills were getting paid. We were staying in decent hotels instead of begging for places to stay. We recorded a new album. In general, we began to experience mostly blessings, which showed me that when we get out of the way and let God be God, he can do so much more than we can do ourselves.

Things these days are totally different and *definitely* better. Owning up to our egotism helped us get past ourselves and kept us from falling deeper into our self-created mess. I'm glad that we had sense enough to claim our part in what was going on instead of pulling the *"Why us, God? What have we done to deserve this?"* card.

Life will always have its ups and downs, but through it all, if we keep God at the forefront and try not to stray away, he'll see us through.

In all your ways acknowledge him, and he will make your paths straight.
—Proverbs 3:6

Joe Nixon
Slick Shoes

05

He is a God of
Wisdom and Patience

"But the wisdom that comes from heaven is first of all pure; then peace-loving, considerate, submissive, full of mercy and good fruit, impartial and sincere."
—**James 3:17**

"The Lord is not slow in keeping his promise, as some understand slowness. He is patient with you, not wanting anyone to perish, but everyone to come to repentance."
—**2 Peter 3:9**

"To God belong wisdom and power; counsel and understanding are his."
—**Job 12:13**

In God I Trust

Trust in the Lord with all your heart and lean not on your own understanding...
—**Proverbs 3:5**

I stood outside the intensive care unit of Hillcrest Hospital, numb with grief. My mind retraced the events of the past few hours: A seemingly simple infection, a necessary I.V., an exam by some experts in white coats with stethoscopes adorning their necks like jewelry. Then came a sudden rush to the intensive care unit. We waited without word. There was unexpected surgery. Her blood pressure dropped. *Code Blue.*

NO! my mind screamed. *Not Code Blue, not her room number, not her!*

Doctors and nurses flooded her room from every direction. So much movement, so much yelling, confusion, turmoil. Then slowly, everyone backed away from the bed where she lay.

My sister had just been pronounced dead.

Not possible, I frantically thought. She was the one I shared a bedroom with for 17 years. Together we had gone to Girl Scout camp, sung for charities, auditioned for the school play, and pulled together lots of last-minute pizza parties in our remodeled basement.

Sometimes we'd get the crazies and pretend to go snipe hunting (something we randomly made up) or round up a bunch of girls with rolls of toilet paper and go mummy up a few houses. One year, we even had a crush on the same guy at the same time. Not cool.

She was the one who was always encouraging me. When I wanted to run for junior class treasurer, she was the first one to start making campaign posters and passing out flyers. When I decided to try out for the Junior Miss scholarship pageant, she listened to me play my guitar, hour after hour, and coached me on my singing. When I went away to New York City to try my luck at modeling, she was forever sending me "follow your dream" letters and little surprises in the mail. Yes, she was my sister, but more importantly, she was my friend.

Now she was gone.

Back at our house, I watched as family and friends started to gather. Some stood crying silently, some were doubled over in agony. Some offered hugs of comfort, some brought food, and others were not sure what to do. Slowly, my numbness turned to simmering disbelief.

God, how could you let this happen? What were you thinking? She was so young. She had so much to live for, I reminded God. *Some things I can let go,* I snapped, *but this one, Lord, you have to explain to me!*

Yet heaven was silent.

Days later, I heard someone say that God does not owe us an explanation for the things that happen in our lives.

That ticked me off. It sounded totally unfair. Of course God owed me an explanation! The rug had been pulled out from underneath my whole life. In fact, I thought that if he were any kind of God at all, he would want to explain the reasons to me—just so that I wouldn't stay angry with him!

But as time wore on, the truth and reality of those words sunk in. Somewhere deep down, I knew they were right. The God of the universe, the same God who created the heavens and the earth, the stars and the sky, the majestic mountains and the miniscule amoebae, didn't have to give me an explanation or run things by me for my permission. After all, he is God: his ways are higher than mine. I could see that I had a choice to make. I could keep giving God the cold shoulder for not playing by my rules, or I could trust him.

I just wasn't ready.

A few weeks after my sister's funeral, I was up in my room reading through some old letters she had sent to me. On the bottom of one of the letters was a P.S. There was a Bible verse written out—a verse from Proverbs. I carefully read the words, "Trust in the Lord with all your heart and lean not on your own understanding."

It was one of her favorites.

I sat there cross-legged on the bedroom floor with a choice to make. Follow my sister's wishes, or remain bitter and angry at God.

I chose to trust God.

I didn't understand, I didn't have all the answers, but I no longer felt like I needed an explanation. I finally let God be God.

With my decision made, my icy attitude toward him began to melt. Then my grief began to ease, just a little. With my thoughts no longer tangled up in the demand for answers, I was free to actually think happy thoughts of my sister and to remember the good times we had.

Good memories of her get me through each day now: memories that I will forever keep tucked inside my trusting heart.

Andrea Stephens

The Age of Silence

Remember not the sins of my youth and my rebellious ways; according to your love remember me, for you are good, O Lord.
—**Psalms 25:7**

Journal entry, July 10:

Troubled teenager. Can anyone define that term? What does it mean, and why are my parents and teachers using that phrase to describe me? I live by my standards and not theirs. I do what I want to do. I am an individual, and I don't care about my parents' opinion. Who are they to tell me how I should live my life? I do what they ask me to. I go to their churches. I attend their schools. I participate in their so-called family outings. So why are they still breathing down my neck to quit smoking? It is my decision, not theirs. Why can't I smoke a little pot here and there? It won't hurt in small quantities. Why does the youth pastor always talk about remaining sex-free until marriage? I have been with my boyfriend for three years, and I might marry him later on down the road anyway. I wish they would just leave me alone.

The summer before my sophomore year in high school I lived the way that I wanted to. I sneaked out at night in order to go to concerts my parents didn't approve of. I partied every weekend, which included drinking and drugs and getting too deep in the relationship with my boyfriend, David. It wasn't long before it caught up with me.

Through the events that happened the few months after I wrote that journal entry, I began to understand why my parents, teachers, and pastor had tried to reach out to me and show me a different path in life. It was not because they did not want me to have fun, or because they wanted me to be exactly like them. They simply loved me and wanted the best for my life.

When school started in September, I wasn't able to keep up with my friends. I was always tired, and even the thought of smoking a cigarette made me nauseated. After school I would no longer hang out at "Stoner Park"— instead I would go home and take a nap. In October, I started to gain a little weight, but I thought that it was just because I was lazy. When I got the flu and started throwing up every morning, I realized that my medical condition could possibly not be the flu. I might be pregnant. I took two home pregnancy tests just to verify my hunch.

I was right.

I felt helpless, confused, and angry. I wondered why this had happened to me. My boyfriend and I hadn't been talking much lately. He lived two hours away, and once school had started, it had been harder for us to see each other. I didn't know who to tell or what to do.

I ended up calling my youth pastor at church and just crying. He remained calm and told me that I had to tell my parents. That was the *last* thing that I wanted to hear. Both of my parents were respected people of the community, leaders in the church, and highly involved in school issues. At first I thought, *They'll kill me.* Then I thought, *How can I ruin their reputation? This will break their hearts.*

I waited a couple of days but I could no longer hide my morning sickness. I told my stepmom first, and then she told my dad. I called my real mom and told her. My mother was angry and terrified about what was going to happen. My father was very quiet and hurt. He stayed up for two nights in silence, reading his Bible and praying.

A week later, my stepmother took me to an organization for pregnant teens callead Crisis Pregnancy Center. They went over the options and counseled me through my decision. Because of my beliefs, abortion was out of the question. They offered me a third option, instead of abortion or becoming a teen mom—adoption. It didn't feel right for me to put my own feelings of wanting to have a baby over my child's right to a happy and successful life. I knew in my heart that I could not give this child the home it deserved—two parents, a stable income, and a safe environment. I just couldn't provide those things.

My dad was glad that I chose adoption, and he did what he could to support me in my decision. On the other hand, my mom thought that I should keep the child. She even offered to help raise it. She was so adamant in her opinion that she tried to take legal action to gain custody of the unborn baby. Luckily, California laws guarded me against her request. My father's parents were so angry that they wouldn't speak to me. Through all of this, I had to stand by my decision to do what I believed in my heart to be right.

The next few months were probably the worst of my life. David stopped talking to me. Being 15 and a father-to-be was probably not easy for him. School became a daily battlefield, as I had to defend myself to my friends. Everyone had his or her own opinion on what I should do.

People would ask me, "Why don't you love your child?" "How can you give him away if you love him?" "If you can't afford to raise him, why don't you take the father to court and make him pay for it? It was his decision, too." Others asked, "How will you know that the people who take your baby won't be freaks who will mentally destroy him?"

Questions like these haunted me as I walked through the halls at school.

I lost almost all of my friends. It wasn't that they didn't like me, but I just couldn't keep up with them anymore. I couldn't stay up past 9:00 p.m. My body wouldn't let me. I couldn't smoke, drink, or mosh in the pits at punk-rock concerts. Everyone lost interest in me.

Being a normal 15-year-old was not an option anymore. I started homeschool in order to make time for all the doctor appointments. I had to eat right, which meant no more fast food. I had to forget about clothing styles and that cute dress in a size four. Oversized t-shirts and stretch pants filled my closet. Instead of Friday nights at the movies, I had Lamaze class with my parents. My life changed dramatically.

I now refer to this period in my life as "The Age of Silence." For maybe the first time in my life, I was able to be silent enough to find out what was truly in my heart, and that was what I needed most. I wanted my unborn son to know who his mother really was, so I began a journal to him.

Keeping the journal helped me to be able to see what I had become. I was amazed at what came to the surface once I was still enough to listen.

I realized that looks and trends were not as important as what was on the inside. I started to change my perspective and the way I looked at people. The friends that I used to have were only concerned about having fun. My true friends ended up being the ones who stood by me and did things with me at my speed, things that I was capable of doing. I started to learn about true love, faith in genuine people, and respect for others.

This new perspective gave me guidelines in choosing new parents for my son. I made a list of all the qualities I had ever wanted in a parent, and I stuck to that list while I was looking for a family. I found a wonderful couple who had been trying to have children for seven years. In the very beginning of the adoption process we chose to have an open adoption so that I could still see my son and talk to the family as he grew older. They helped me emotionally, financially, and spiritually as we went through the pregnancy together.

I visited the adoptive parents, Joe and Christine, in Washington, and they flew to California to stay at my family's house. Christine lived with me until I gave birth, and she was even allowed to cut the umbilical cord in the delivery room. When it was time for them to go back home after Isaac was born, I was sad to see them leave because we had become so close.

Some people ask me how I could have given my child away. I do not see it that way. I see it as giving the gift of life. I feel so lucky to have been able to bless people with something they had always wanted but could never have. I wanted Isaac to have a life full of love—not heartache. I wanted to give my child everything that he could ever want even if that meant being raised by someone other than me.

Within that nine-month period I changed from a harsh, confused "troubled teenager" into someone who knows what she stands for. I am a person who appreciates life and has a heart of love. I know the importance of surrounding myself with real people and real friends. Now I have confidence in who I am, and that is more valuable than anything else I have ever known. My relationship with my parents has dramatically changed. We do not see eye-to-eye all the time, but our respect for each other has been strengthened.

I am now finishing up my teen years as a student at Vanguard University and working a job at a pharmacy. I still go to rock concerts and stay up late, and I take time to do other things that I enjoy. I would never have had this opportunity if I had made a different choice and kept Isaac. Joe and Christine send me pictures every few months, and I talk to them on the phone regularly.

The list of qualities that I made while looking for that special family is taped to the inside of my journal. I still read it and pray that someday I will be a mom—when the time is right—and that I will become a woman of virtue that my son or daughter can admire.

Leah C. Koop

Traveling on the Same Track

Keep yourselves in God's love as you wait for the mercy of our Lord Jesus Christ to bring you to eternal life.
—Jude 1:21

It was the middle of my freshman year, and I was a new student. I sat alone, as usual, during the dreaded lunch hour and watched Philip, with his strange lunging stride, walk into a cluster of students. They smiled and said, "How goes it, Philip?" When he answered, his words came out slowly. They didn't wait to listen. As if they had some important place to be, they hurried away. "See ya, Philip."

Before the accident, he was a star athlete. Football, track, wrestling—Philip did it all. After the car wreck, Philip's arm didn't move unless he lifted it with his other hand. His rigid right leg was in a brace, but he could walk using two canes.

The one thing I shared in common with Philip is that no one wanted to hang out with me, either. Usually at lunch he'd sit down next to me. When he spoke, his voice shook, and I knew it was an effort for him to make his words clear. Because speech didn't come easily, he didn't waste words. He expressed his thoughts like a poet. He said things like, "Even the stars know we are here."

I no longer dreaded lunchtime. I liked Philip's company.

But then one afternoon everything changed. I was in the girls' restroom when someone, not knowing I was in the stall, started talking. "Looks like Philip's got a girlfriend. Did you notice her dress? It was mine. I gave it to Goodwill last year."

Then another voice said, "Once upon a time, Philip wouldn't have been seen dead with her, but now he's brain-damaged. It's lucky for both of them that they found each other."

A different voice said, "Do you think... oh, you know." They giggled.

The next day Philip and I were studying together, and I noticed some girls looking in our direction. Painfully self-conscious, I began to avoid Philip, and I spent lunch hour in the library.

I even stopped riding home on the school bus. Mornings were bad enough, but afternoons were the worst. When I got on the bus and started to sit down, someone always put a hand on the seat and said, "Saved." Every day I walked home. It made my Aunt Hanna upset, but her anger was easier to handle than the bus.

It took about an hour to walk home. Most of the time, Aunt Hanna wasn't there. But one afternoon she was.

When I walked up to the house with no bus in sight, she grabbed my shoulders, shook me, and scolded, "I told you to ride on that bus. What have you been doing? Been with some boy? What are you? Some kind of tramp? If it weren't for me, you'd be in a foster home. This is the appreciation I get!"

That night I was so mad at Aunt Hanna I couldn't sleep. I thought about the movie I had seen where people during the Depression jumped onto freight trains to travel to California and pick fruit. The thought of leaving all those horrible girls and Aunt Hanna behind made me jump out of bed. I searched for a pair of scissors, and when I found them, without hesitation I angled them just below my right ear. Snip. A chunk of hair fell into my lap. Before I knew it, the majority of my hair was on the floor. *Good,* I thought. *Now I won't match the description Aunt Hanna will give once she realizes that I'm gone.*

I crept into the kitchen, grabbed some canned food, and threw it, along with a change of clothes, into my backpack. Then I opened the window, perched on the ledge, and leaped down to the street. I ran quickly, like smoke freed from a smoldering fire.

Thunder suddenly cracked. Rain began to fall. By the time I reached the industrial area and could see train tracks reflecting the yellow streetlight, I was soaking wet. Exhausted, I sank down in the shelter of the railroad platform. All the previous excitement and visions of adventure drained away. I felt empty and desolate. I'd never been so lonely. Self-pity hit as suddenly as the rain stopped. Believing that no one was within earshot, I yelled out into the night, cursing and crying.

Suddenly, I heard a cough. Heart thumping, I jumped to my feet. Someone stood in the doorway of the entrance of the train station.

"Hi Mister." I made my voice low, like I was a boy.

He didn't answer. Instead he cupped his hands to his mouth and started playing a harmonica. I'll never forget the sound he made: its powerful, sorrowful beauty. Struck by a kind of awe, I walked up to him. He kept playing.

Then he stopped. "I lost my boy. Died in my arms. So cold in the boxcar. Freezing. My boy got pneumonia. Hospitals didn't treat homeless boys with no insurance. Died in my arms. My boy died in my arms."

It was hard to hear him tell about his son. It wasn't long ago that the paper had a story about a woman who drove her car off a bridge. The car was sinking. She climbed up on top of it. She begged the people on the bridge to help her, but the car went under. No one tried to save her.

That's like me, I thought. I was embarrassed when people were saying things about me and Philip, and no one stepped in to help or defend me. I gave up being with someone I really liked just because no one cared about Philip or me enough to rescue us from the torment of calloused high school girls.

I don't know how long I stood on the railroad platform. But as I walked back home, the sun was starting to rise. Everything had shifted. I just didn't know it yet. I've heard it said that if you change your angle of vision just a tiny bit, everything changes. That's what happened; I began to see things differently.

As I came up the street, I saw Aunt Hanna standing on the front porch. She never went outside without getting dressed, makeup and all. But there she was in her robe, hair all messed up. I knew she'd been crying. I walked up on the porch. No matter how much she yelled and carried on, I could see past her words into her heart. For the first time, I realized she got upset with me because she loved me.

The next day at school, I sat down next to Philip. He laughed when he saw my hair. I told him how I had cut it off to run away, and I told him what had happened at the train station. "Just before I started walking back home, Philip, the man I was telling you about said, 'Remember this one thing: there's a train going to the east and a train going to the west, but they all travel on the same track. Folks are like trains. They travel on the same track.' What do you think he meant?"

"Maybe," Philip said, "people think they're alone. But no matter how anyone looks, no matter what they believe, or how rich or poor, everybody is traveling on the same track, and that track is God's love."

I knew Philip would know.

Patricia Hathaway Breed

The Only True Peacemaker

And the peace of God, which transcends all under-standing, will guard your hearts and your minds in Christ Jesus.
—**Philippians 4:7**

A sense of dread came over me, and I automatically grabbed my friend's wet sleeve and pulled her toward the house. "Tara, let's get up on the front porch," I urged. It was almost as though God was warning me, *Hey Adrianne, you may want to get out of the line of fire.*

Tara and I were outside playing around in the warm rain of a tropical summer storm when I saw her ex-boyfriend, Ray, come out of his house with something wrapped up in a towel.

I had shrugged off the warning of a friend of Ray's who had called just half an hour before. "Ray is looking for a gun. He's really upset, and I think he might be planning to do something bad," the friend had warned.

"What's he gonna do? Assassinate me? *Please!*"

In my 13-year-old mind, there was no way that Ray would intentionally try to hurt us. He lived just down the street, and I had known him for years before he and Tara began going out. She was 15—he was 20.

It wasn't always easy being his friend. Outside of people in our neighborhood, Ray mostly connected with gang members. His life had been hard. When Ray was only seven, he had seen his father killed, and since that time, neither his mother nor his brothers ever showed love to him. I believe that contributed to his violence.

I took him to church now and then—Ray and lots of others from the neighborhood who didn't have a church or any relationship with God. Tara came pretty often. She was there the day that I formally gave my life to God.

Now Tara had broken up with Ray, and he was very hurt about the whole thing. He felt that I would abandon him too, I guess, since Tara and I were friends. Being rejected by Tara and thinking he was losing my friendship in the process turned out to be more than he could handle.

Just as we reached the steps of the porch, it felt like an impact of air went through my back. In that moment, the very wind was stolen from my life and I would never be the same again; I would never regain my innocence.

"Mom, help!" I screamed. "Ray shot me!"

My mom was home, thank God, as was my big brother, Jeremy. He should have been at one of his college classes, but his professor had let them go early that day. I don't know what I would have done without either of them. Mom heard me scream, and she ran out and got

Tara and me into the house. I was lying on the living room floor when suddenly Ray opened the front door. Luckily, Jeremy had come out of his room just in time to throw all his weight against the door and lock it.

That didn't stop Ray. He came in through the back door—Jeremy thought he had locked it, but he hadn't.

My mom was in the kitchen dialing 911. Whether he was trying to stop her from getting help or she was simply in his path, Ray began to fire at my mom, shooting her in the wrist and arm and then twice in the chest. In an instant, Ray was towering over her with the gun pointed at her head, and she was asking God if she was going to live. Suddenly, she felt a sense of peace come over her, and she regained enough courage to pin the gun against the doorframe and stand up.

Just then, Jeremy appeared, and they both attempted to wrestle the gun away from Ray, but Ray maintained control enough to put the gun into his mouth, claiming that he wanted to kill himself.

At that moment, my mom's thoughts were for Ray to just go ahead and do it—to free everyone, including himself, from this pain and trauma. But instead she blurted out, "Ray, if you kill yourself, you'll never find forgiveness, and you'll go to hell."

Incredibly, that got through to him, and he dropped the gun.

The police finally arrived after things had calmed down, and they took Ray off to jail. Mom and I were taken to the hospital.

The gunshot missed my spine by only an inch, saving me from being paralyzed. My mom and I both survived the attack without any major complications. Luckily, Tara and Jeremy made it through without any gunshot wounds.

Once I was healing, I thought that things would settle down, but instead they got more difficult. Surviving the attack by Ray was my first hurdle; the next one came out of the blue and as a total shock. Ray had gone to jail, but that didn't stop Tara from getting in touch with him. She began building her relationship with him again by phone, and what happened next threw me into a downward spiral of depression and confusion.

I went to call Tara one afternoon only to find that my phone number had been blocked from her phone. All trust that I had flew out the window. How could my friend, with whom I survived nearly getting killed, befriend our attacker and betray me? To say the least, my innocence was shattered, and my ability to trust people had blown away like that summer storm.

The three years ahead would prove just how profoundly my life had been changed by the trauma. I endured nightmares for six months after the attack. I continually struggled with feelings of anger and hate. It was soon apparent that my personality was no longer the same. I had once loved being outdoors and spent most of my spare time outside. Now I seldom went outside except to get from one place to another. Also, I was afraid of the dark—of the unknown. Jeremy had to sleep in my room for an entire year.

I no longer trusted men, and although I was still too young to date anyone, I didn't have any casual crushes nor would I even entertain the idea of "going out" with someone. I made friends easily, as I had always been an outgoing person. But none of the friendships I had were anything but casual. Having at least one true friend would have done wonders to help me get through the hard moments.

I just couldn't get past the enormous sense of betrayal that followed the events of that summer afternoon. Often alone and isolated by choice, I had just lost faith in the human race. I never lost faith in God, though—I remained connected to him enough to keep going to my church group.

One night, as I was lying on the floor of the house where we were meeting, I was dwelling on how lonely and isolated I had felt for so long. It was finally getting to me. My heart was telling my mind that it couldn't shove these feelings into a deep, dark place anymore. I began to realize that God could free me from this sad place and help me find my way to trusting and relating to others again. The next thought was that God was speaking to me, asking me to simply ask for his help. I was so distraught, so ready to give this burden over, I replied, *Okay, help me, God.*

Suddenly, I started crying. The anguish of those three years came pouring out, and at the same time I felt a genuine sense of peace. Still, I didn't notice that any real change had occurred within me until the next day.

A family friend stopped by our house to bring my mom some plants. It was a very hot afternoon, and as he stood on the porch outside the front door, I invited him in for a cold drink. He immediately realized that there was something very different going on with me. Knowing me through the years, he had been a recipient of my "cold shoulder" approach to men. I would never have invited him inside if I weren't changed in a significant way.

It was at that moment that I knew God was healing me, and that I was not the same as I had been the night before. I realized that I was no longer angry or hurt at Ray or Tara. All along, I had been holding God partly responsible for letting that terrible incident happen. But once I asked him to help me, I felt him saying, *I never took my hand off you. It's all still okay.*

I knew that I had finally been restored to the more trusting, happy person that I once had been. The storm had finally blown over. I was able to make peace with my past.

After all the struggles that I went through, I now realize that God is the only true peacemaker. I know firsthand what his love and grace can do.

Adrianne Webster

How Sweet the Sound

May the Lord direct your hearts into God's love...
—**2 Thessalonians 3:5**

The lead should have been mine. All my friends agreed with me.

At least, it shouldn't have been Tiffany's, that weird new girl. She never had a word to say, always looking down at her feet as if her life were too heavy to bear. What was up with that? We'd never done anything to her. We began to think that she was just stuck up, because with all the great clothes she wore, things couldn't have been that bad for her. I bet she never had on the same thing more than twice in the two months she'd been at our school.

The worst of it was when she showed up at play try-outs and sang for my part. Everyone knew the lead role was meant for me. After all, I had parts in all our high school musicals, and this was our senior year.

My friends were waiting, so I didn't bother to hang around for Tiffany's audition. The shock came two days later when we hurried to check the drama department bulletin board for the cast postings. We scanned the sheets looking for my name. When we found it, I burst out in tears. Tiffany had gotten the lead! I was cast as her mother and her understudy. *Understudy?* Nobody could believe it.

Rehearsals seemed to go on forever. Tiffany didn't appear to notice that we were going out of our way to ignore her.

I admit it: Tiffany did have a beautiful voice. I also noticed that she was somehow different on stage. Not so much happy as settled and content.

Opening night we all had jitters. Everyone was quietly bustling around backstage, waiting for the curtain to go up—everyone but Tiffany, of course. She seemed contained in her own calm world.

The performance was a hit. Our timing was perfect; our voices blended and soared. Tiffany and I flowed back and forth, weaving the story between us. I was the ailing mother praying for her wayward daughter, and Tiffany played the daughter who realizes as her mother dies that there is more to life than *this* life.

The final scene reached its dramatic end. I was lying in the darkened bedroom. The prop bed I was on was uncomfortable, making it hard to stay still. I was impatient, anxious for Tiffany's big finish to be over.

She was spotlighted upstage, the grieving daughter beginning to understand the true meaning of the hymn she had been singing as her mother passed away.

"Amazing grace, how sweet the sound..." Her voice lifted over the pain of her mother's death and the joy of God's promises.

"...that saved a wretch like me..." Something real was happening to me as Tiffany sang. My impatience began to melt away.

"...I once was lost but now I'm found..." My heart was suddenly moved to tears.

"...was blind but now I see." My spirit began to come alive within me and I found myself turning to God. In that moment, it was as if I knew his love, his desire for me, for the first time.

Tiffany's voice lingered in the prayer of the last note. The curtain dropped. Complete silence. Not a sound.

Tiffany stood behind the closed curtain, head bowed, gently weeping. Suddenly applause and cheers erupted, and when the curtain parted, Tiffany saw the standing ovation.

We all made our final bows, and then I turned and gave Tiffany a genuine hug. Everyone broke off in their usual groups, congratulating each other—everyone but Tiffany and me.

"Tiffany, your song—it was so real for me." I hesitated, my feelings intense. "You sang me into the heart of God."

Tiffany gasped. Her eyes met mine. "That's what my mother said to me the night she died." A tear slipped down her cheek. "She was in such pain, but when I sang 'Amazing Grace,' it always comforted her. She said I should always remember that God has promised good to me and that his grace would lead her home."

I began to understand why Tiffany always seemed sad—and so quiet.

Her face was lit from the inside out, her mother's love shining through. "The night she died she whispered to me, 'Sing me into the heart of God, Tiffany.' That night and tonight, I sang for her."

Cynthia M. Hamond, S.F.O.

My Mountaintop Experience

Do not judge, or you too will be judged. For in the same way you judge others, you will be judged, and with the measure you use, it will be measured to you.
—**Matthew 7:1-2**

I focused on the top of the hill, and I climbed. For a weeklong retreat, this was serious work. My legs felt like jelly, and my pack felt as though someone had filled it with rocks while I slept. I tried to look up at the majestic view of the mountains surrounding me, but my head swam from the altitude, so I concentrated on not tumbling down the hill.

Just out of sight was my group, chock-full of hungry football players. Thus far the trip had been a bust. This was our second day on the mountain, and it was obvious that the boys were simply here for the training, not for the spiritual awakening I had anticipated. I hated feeling their eyes on me as I brought up the rear, every time, as though I were nothing more than an inconvenience to them on the mountain. If we were up here in order to strengthen relationships, you could have fooled me. There could be six inches between us around the campfire, and they would still be a million miles away.

I returned to these mountains every year just for the experience—a chance to bond with nature and friends and to rekindle my fire for spirituality that tended to fade during the year. Every year I loaded the bus, eager to carry a 40-pound pack and sleep under the stars. I longed for the chance to revel in God's unaltered perfection.

But on no other trip had 40 pounds felt so heavy, and never before had such a shadow been cast on God's glorious mountains. The focus had veered from embracing the journey to racing to the destination. I didn't think the boys would notice if we had been hiking through a mini-mart parking lot. God had been lost between the grunts and burps of the immature members of the group.

I huffed and puffed up to a half-buried boulder and rested the weight of my pack on it as I gazed down the incline. I watched Abbey labor up the hill, farther down. As I watched her trudge up the hill, I chugged some water and tried to regain my motivation to reach the top and join the rest of the group.

Suddenly, Abbey sank to her knees. I unclipped my pack and half-walked, half-rolled down the hill to her.

I heard her wheezing and coughing as I approached. I pulled her pack off and lodged it between two rocks. She rolled onto her back and stared up into the crystal blue skies of the Colorado Rockies.

"Abbey!" I cried, "Say something!"

She looked at me, gasping for air, "Asthma… attack…"

I screamed down the hill for my trail guide, who was still a ways away. I tried to speak, but only fragments came out.

"John, help me! Abbey! Asthma!"

He waltzed up the hill toward us as though this were just a stroll in the park. He rested his pack next to us and examined Abbey carefully.

"Abbey, have you ever had an asthma attack before?" he asked. She shook her head weakly as her chest heaved with every struggling breath. He turned to me. "She'll be fine," he assured. "Continue up the hill—it's not that far. The others should be waiting at the top. Send Chuck back down."

I nodded weakly and tried to run up the hill to my pack. I watched John sit Abbey up and talk to her as I lifted my pack onto my back. I turned up the hill and started hiking. My breath was weak and short, but I knew I did not have the luxury of stopping for breaks any longer. I distracted myself by counting my steps, singing songs we had learned in youth group, and remembering all the talks Abbey and I had had on the two-day bus trip from Ohio. As the boys came into view I tried to speed up, but I could no longer feel my legs and didn't seem to be making any progress.

As I approached the group I knew the boys wouldn't care unless it involved food or some testosterone-based activity, so I tried to ignore their looks as I searched for Chuck. He stood about a head shorter than all of them but was incredibly fit as a trail guide and therefore had no trouble keeping up with the hulks on the trail. I dropped my pack with the others and looked up into Chuck's friendly face, but again, only fragments emerged from my mouth as I tried to regain my composure in the high altitude.

"John, Abbey, asthma attack."

That was all Chuck needed; he shot some directions at us to stay put, but they were carried off by the wind, and he was gone over the crest of the hill.

I sank onto the rock in Chuck's place and curled up to shield myself from the brunt of the wind. I felt a tap on my shoulder.

"Emily, hey, Em!" I opened my eyes to see Matt looking inquisitively at me. "Is she okay?" he asked.

I was stunned. Was I hearing intelligible speech coming from this boy? Did he actually care about the welfare of someone else with no personal gain for himself? I looked around and saw that the same look was mirrored on the other four boys' faces. I looked back at Matt; they were actually worried.

"Uh, yeah, she'll be fine, I think." I stammered. This calmed them only slightly. Was I hearing things? I doubted their sincerity, quite honestly. I assured myself that they were only worried because waiting for Abbey was slowing them down. These boys cared only about themselves, not what happened to Abbey and me.

Jimmy stood up quickly. "It's Chuck!" he shouted, and pointed as Chuck emerged over the crest of the hill. He was alone but carrying something. All of us watched as he dropped Abbey's 40-pound pack at our feet as though it were empty.

The boys looked at each other and all stood up. I watched them gather around the pack. *What are they doing?* I asked myself.

BJ gathered their five packs and dragged them over. I heard the sound of zippers as they worked. Occasionally I would hear pieces of their conversation shouted over the wind. "I can fit that in mine, Sam!" or "My pack is full; what can I tie to the outside?"

It dawned on me: they were planning to carry the weight of Abbey's pack for her. They wanted to make the trip easier for her, so, without any prompting or suggestion, they were taking her burden on themselves. I looked over at Chuck, who was smiling at their good deed.

Donald turned to me as the boys continued working. He eyed my pack and said quietly, "Hey Em, I noticed you were having trouble back there"—he gestured back down the hill—"and I still have room in my pack. If you want, I can take some of the weight for you."

I sighed and smiled back at him, saying "Sure, thanks." I opened my pack and gave him some of my gear, imagining how much easier this would make the hike. I watched him walk away as the boys finished with Abbey's pack. They had left only the frame with one pocket still full.

As they backed away, we all watched John escort Abbey over the hill and to the rock. She looked very pale, and she eyed the beaming boys and her empty pack warily. John helped her sit down next to me on the rock. She looked at me questioningly, and I smiled back at her. "The boys are going to carry your stuff for you," I explained.

She looked at them, and they blushed. Sam stepped forward. "We figured it would help since you're feeling sick. We left your personal stuff; your toothbrush and stuff..." His voice trailed off as he smiled shyly.

Abbey smiled back. "Thanks, guys."

The group rested for a while, and I finally had the chance to admire the wonders around me: not just the magnificent view, but the wondrous people as well. These were not the boys I knew from school, and these were not the boys with whom I had started the hike.

Something had changed.

As we put our packs back on, the sky looked a little bluer, the air was a little fresher, and I had no trouble watching the scenery instead of the ground. We approached the rocky ridge that was to be our next challenge, but I was not fearful at all. Instead of lagging behind, Abbey and I were in the midst of the huge football players, who no longer seemed so big, who no longer seemed so distant. The attitude of the entire group had improved. We were less weary, less anxious, less a collection of individuals and more the group none of us had thought possible. Chuck walked next to me for a while, observing our new attitude.

"God touches everyone on the mountain," he said. "I guess even these boys have hearts."

He grinned as I realized that I, too, had been changed by this experience. Atop that mountain the Holy Spirit flowed among us and gave us all an awakening which no one could have expected.

Emily Smith, 16

Speaking Up

I do not hide your righteousness in my heart; I speak of your faithfulness and salvation. I do not conceal your love and your truth from the great assembly.
—Psalms 40:10

I have always been a people pleaser. I have always tried to fit in, to be one of the crowd.

At school I was everybody's friend. I fit in with the Preps and the Goths and every other stereotype you can imagine. It seemed to me that everybody else had something I wanted. No matter what I did, I couldn't find it.

I have gone to church just about my whole life. I sang the songs and talked the talk, but I never really bought into it. I always thought that since other people in my family believed, I didn't have to—I was covered. I loved going to church and hanging out with my friends on Sundays, but on Monday I was the girl who always fit in.

About God I always thought, *How I am I supposed to love a person I don't know?* Like if someone said to you, "I know a guy, and he's madly in love with you. Don't you love him, too?" If you had any common sense, you'd want to know who the person was—at least I did.

People always say, "I found Jesus." That's not how it was for me. I didn't find anything, no matter how hard I looked. The bottom line is that Jesus came looking for me. Don't get me wrong—it wasn't like, "Oh, I know Jesus now," and everything was all hearts and flowers. I wish it worked that way.

But about a year and half ago, I started to run after God for real.

Some of my friends from church talked me into going to a conference with them, and one of the speakers talked about how if you fit in perfectly with the world, you have a problem. I didn't think of it as a problem. I just thought the speaker didn't have any friends in high school and was still bitter about it. The other speakers were all about change-the-world-this and change-the-world-that. I was doing just fine in my little corner of the world not changing anything. They weren't hitting me like a lightning bolt: boom, change the world for Jesus.

Then over the weekend I was praying one of my packaged prayers: you know, "Bless Mom, bless Dad, thanks for everything I own, it would be nice to have world peace while you're at it." But during my prayer, the speaker's voice kept playing in my head. It hit me that out of all the people I knew, maybe two knew I was a Christian.

I'm always trying to fit in—not make waves, I thought. *Exactly what kind of impact am I making?* I knew if I were to speak up, people would look at me like I'd escaped from a place with padded walls—but if I didn't, then one day I'd have to try to explain to God that I was too embarrassed to let people know that I loved him. I didn't want to have to imagine that.

So I switched off of my "bless everyone" prayer and began to talk to God for real. I asked for boldness and courage every night, but in the morning I didn't wake up feeling like Wonder Woman.

Then I remembered how my older sister once told me that courage only comes after you face what you fear. You have to challenge your fears in order to defeat them.

I decided to speak up about my faith, although I knew that it wouldn't be easy for me. I was really scared of what people would think. Remember, I had never been an individual; I had always tried to blend in. It was a huge stretch for me. It is never easy being the only one standing for what you believe.

I discovered that my sister was right. After I told one person what I believed, telling one more wasn't difficult. Believe it or not, other people saw that I was making a stand for Jesus, and they stood up right next to me.

For the first time in my life, I didn't try to fit in with anyone. In the process, I lost some of my friends because of my honesty. But faithful to the end, God soon sent good, strong Christian friends—people I didn't know well and really didn't want to know at first, I'll admit. Now that they are my friends, I see how judgmental and wrong I was. I would have missed so much not really knowing them.

Things are not easy; I don't think they ever will be. There are times when I know I am supposed to witness, but I back out. I kick myself for it, but I know that God forgives me every time. He's working with me.

I no longer fit in with every group, but how can you be passionately in love with Jesus and still play the field? You can't. If it comes down to a choice between "be welcomed on this earth" or "be welcomed in heaven," I will choose heaven any day.

Lauren Alyson Schara, 16

Changes

"... Return to me, and I will return to you," says the Lord Almighty...
—**Malachi 3:7**

Having surfed most of my life, I had always wanted to share my faith in a more powerful way with other surfers. God had given me so much that I wanted others to know the peace and fulfillment that I got through my relationship with him.

One day, God gave me the idea to create a video that included the testimonies of some professional surfers who were also believers. With help from some surf and skate companies and a few others who shared the vision, the video was made. We titled it *Changes*.

We put a lot of prayer and preparation into the project, hoping that it would change lives in a significant way. We knew that if we let God work through us, he would make things happen that we could never even dream of. That's exactly what he did.

We went to Japan to film the movie, and while there, I really developed a heart for the Japanese people. Only a very small number of Japanese believe in Jesus. I saw that they didn't have the Lord, and it broke my heart. I wanted to reach out to them with the gospel.

Once the video was finished, we showed it in just about every city in California and in other parts of the U.S., too. For some reason, Japan kept coming up. Still, we didn't understand what we were supposed to do about it.

Then, out of the blue, God dropped a lady named Emi into our lives. She lived right down the street but was originally from Japan. Emi loved surfing—and God. To our amazement, she got behind the project and flew over to Japan to set up a trip for us. She even translated the video into Japanese.

Soon we were on our way back to Japan to see what God had in store for us.

Skip Frye and Mitch Abshire, two famous longboarders, came along on this mission. We were met at the Tokyo airport by representatives of a longboarder magazine. They were doing a story on us and had scheduled a photo shoot at a beach about an hour and a half away.

I ended up in a car driven by the main editor, a guy named Steve. Since we were there to share the video and our faith, I decided to share my testimony with him about how I became a Christian. Steve spoke English since he'd lived in Hawaii, so luckily I didn't need a translator. As I talked away, he glanced at me, carefully taking his eyes off the road just long enough to acknowledge that he was listening. I couldn't tell what he was thinking—whether I was annoying him or if he was really interested.

As I finished my story, I looked over at him and was blown away by what I saw. There he was, driving along, with tears splashing down on his t-shirt and board shorts. I thought, *What's happening here?* I hadn't expected my testimony to affect him that way.

He turned again and looked my way for a second. "I just want you to know," he began, "that I believe that God brought you here today."

I didn't get it.

He explained that his mother had been diagnosed with terminal cancer and that he'd been struggling with the question of where God was in the midst of all their suffering and heartache. Just the day before, the doctor had told him that his mom had only about two months to live, but he hadn't told her the news yet.

It was so overwhelming to hear this. I couldn't think of anything to say that would be right in the situation, so I asked if I could pray for him. I put my hand on his shoulder, and as I prayed, I felt as if God were telling me to ask him if we could visit his mom. So I asked.

A look of total bewilderment came across his face. He seemed to be thinking to himself, *Why is this guy even considering taking time on his trip to visit a dying woman he doesn't even know?*

He shook his head and said, "Wow, that would be great. But why would you want to do that? Didn't you guys come to Japan to surf?"

"Actually, we came to Japan to share our movie, and the movie is about the gospel of Jesus. That's why we're here. We've been praying for three months about this trip. We came over here to help people and to love people," I assured him.

"Would Skip want to come?" he asked. "Didn't he come here to surf?"

"We're here to serve the Lord, and that's what we're ready to do," I countered. "He'll come."

He called his mom to see if she was up to having a bunch of surfers drop by for a visit. She said that she'd like that. So we went surfing, took the photos for the article, and then went to Steve's house.

We pulled up to their amazing Japanese home. After taking our shoes off, we walked into a room where a beautiful older Japanese woman awaited us. It's hard to explain her beauty. Something shone through her, even though she was obviously very sick and sat with tubes in her nose. She hadn't been told the bad news from her doctor and still had hope that she would be able to beat the cancer.

When we came in, her eyes lit up, and a huge smile spread across her face. Japanese people are usually pretty reserved and formal people, so her response was unusual. We were thinking, *Here she is, dying of cancer, and she's beaming with beauty and joy.*

Skip sat down next to her and began to talk with the help of a translator. Skip is in his sixties and was the closest in age to Steve's mother, so we let him take the lead. He signed some photos of him surfing, which we weren't sure meant as much to her as to her son, since he definitely knew who Skip was in the world of surfing. Steve was still wondering why a couple of professional surfers were doing all this. He couldn't comprehend why we would even care.

Then Skip asked through the translator if he could pray for her. She accepted. We kept wondering why she seemed so happy about a visit from three surfers she had never met—why she was so receptive to our attention and prayers.

When we returned to the United States a few days later, I e-mailed Steve to ask how his mom was doing and to thank him for everything.

His answer came back a few hours later. He wrote that the day before we arrived in Japan, his mother learned that she would have to have a CAT scan at the hospital and was very scared to go though the procedure. She had told him that for the first time in 20 years, she had wanted to pray. But since she didn't feel worthy to come before God because she had ignored him for so long, she didn't allow herself to pray.

Steve wrote that while his mother was growing up in Hawaii, she had gone to a school where she had learned about Jesus. She knew who Christ was, but she just couldn't believe that he would be happy to hear from her after all this time. But when three Christian men showed up the next day, she felt like it had been a sign from God, that he had known her need to connect with him. She didn't really care who we were—just that we had come to pray for her when she couldn't do it for herself.

Since the number of Christians in Japan is so small, it really couldn't have happened any other way. It blew us away when we realized that God had sent us there to be his hands and feet thousands of miles away from home. He totally orchestrated the whole connection.

Steve also wrote that after we left, he could sense that her life had been changed in a very big way. At a very hard time in her life, she was reminded that Jesus loved and cared about her. God was responding to her through us by saying, *I have not forgotten you. I don't care if it's been 20 years or 50 years, you can always come back to me and I'll hear your prayers.* She must have been comforted to know that.

Bryan Jennings

Out of the Muck

He lifted me out of the slimy pit, out of the mud and mire; he set my feet on a rock and gave me a firm place to stand.
—Psalms 40:2

I have two memories from the time when my parents were still married.

One is of the time when my dad pushed our car through the Pennsylvania snow to safety. Even though I was less than four years old, I knew that he was my hero.

The other memory I have is of a day when Dad was drunk. He was so out of control that he punched a hole in the wall of the house. He broke his arm. The next thing I knew, my mom was carrying me down the dark street with no shoes on. I don't remember ever going back to that house. After that, we moved to Florida, away from Dad.

Thus began the lifelong tension in my heart between the hero and the drunk.

In the coming years I spent a lot of time with Dad on the road. He would drive all the way to Florida to pick me up and take me back to his house in Pennsylvania. All the way there, he would ask me to hand him "road cokes" out of the cooler. I knew these drinks would change my dad, but I didn't know I needed to confront him about it—not yet.

At 15 years old, Jesus called me to be a Christian. I was hard to reach because I admired my dad so much; he didn't believe in God, so I didn't either. But God got hold of me through other Christians in my school. Then God began calling me to be involved in my dad's life in a new way.

There were two important events in my life that my dad attended—drunk. It took those painful experiences to realize that it was time to be a Christian influence on my dad. At my high school graduation, my father gave his life to Christ as a result of the sobering thoughts of his own father's recent death. The second event was in my new church, when I preached my first sermon. Dad was in the congregation—drunk. I confronted him, and thus began the hard road of tough love.

Some time later, Dad called me and suggested that he make a geographic change and move to Florida. My mentor told me that alcoholics often try to make geographic changes, and he warned that it would not be a good idea to allow Dad to be that close to my family. It was really tough, but I told my father that he could move wherever he wanted, but I would not allow him to live close to his daughter-in-law or grandson until he went to an effective recovery program. I told him about a year-long program called

Teen Challenge in Sanford, Florida. He said he would get back to me.

That same week, Dad got another DUI. He had already gotten several DUIs in two states, even after his driver's license had been taken away. This meant jail time. He lost the executive position that he had held for 28 years. His wife of 22 years filed for divorce. His teenage daughter no longer spoke to him.

Crazy as it sounds, I had been praying for 13 years for this very crisis to happen. My prayers became so desperate that I asked God for him to bottom out—in fact, I asked God to throw him in jail. But I asked that he wouldn't die without knowing God.

Dad finally "got back to me," and this time, his phone call would change both of our lives forever. Instead of agreeing to check into the recovery program, he said, "Brian, when I hang up this phone, I am going to kill myself." I didn't know that he had just duct-taped a vacuum hose to the tailpipe of his Chevy Blazer so that he could die in the garage.

My blood ran cold, and my next thought was to call 911 and catch the next flight to Pennsylvania. Then God gave me something to say that I could only deliver with his strength behind me.

"Dad, before you do that, consider what it will do to your grandson," I said. "It will send him the message that Pikalows quit. It will tell him that suicide is an option, and it will devastate him because everything about you will be lost. He won't know you, or anything you stand for." Finally I just told him I would pray for him, and the phone call was over. It was the hardest thing in the world to hang up not knowing if my dad would choose life or death.

Dad thought about what I had said, and he dropped to his knees. Then he turned everything over to God for the first time in his life.

A few minutes later, he called back and said, "I'll do it. I'll go to the program. What do we do next?"

Since a judge was about to sentence him to jail, Dad had to convince his lawyer, who had never heard of Teen Challenge, to persuade a judge in Pennsylvania to sentence him to sunny Florida for a year there. This was not going to be easy, so I called on Destiny Student Ministries at Pine Castle United Methodist Church in Orlando, Florida, to pray for a miracle in a Pennsylvania courtroom.

The judge asked Dad why he wanted to have such an odd sentence for his crime. Teen Challenge is a very tough program—some say harder than doing jail time. My dad told the judge that he needed to be set free, and that only Jesus could do it. The judge said, "If this is how the gentleman feels about it, the state of Pennsylvania feels the same."

Miracles and restoration started immediately. When I left Dad at the doorstep of Teen Challenge, I had hope for him for the first time in years. Dad says that at the moment we drove away, he felt the words of Psalms 40:2, where it says that God will pull you out of the muck and the mire and set you on the rock of Jesus Christ and give you hope for your life.

Dennis Pikalow was in the Teen Challenge recovery program for 11 months. Four years have gone by, and Dad has become a statistic. He is one of the people who contribute to the Teen Challenge 86% recovery rate, which is the best in the nation. Way to go, Dad!

Way to go, God, for saving the one person I thought would never change. Thank you for giving me the strength to take a stand.

Brian Pikalow

06

He is a God of
Compassion

"But you, O Lord, are a compassionate and gracious God, slow to anger, abounding in love and faithfulness."
—Psalms 86:15

"Yet the Lord longs to be gracious to you; he rises to show you compassion…"
—Isaiah 30:18

"…When he cries out to me, I will hear, for I am compassionate."
—Exodus 22:27

Let Me Say Goodbye

For God does speak—now one way, now another—though man may not perceive it. In a dream, in a vision of the night, when deep sleep falls on men as they slumber in their beds, he may speak in their ears...

—Job 33:14-16

I woke up to my grandma shaking me urgently. Disoriented by the blackness that filled my bedroom, thinking it much too early to rise, I rolled over to go back to sleep. At 14, I hated getting up in the morning. And at this early hour, I didn't see the need.

"I know it's early, Emily," said Grandma. "But there is someone downstairs who needs to talk to you."

At those words I jolted awake, remembering that Dad was out of town and that I expected news about him. Mom had flown to Chicago earlier in the week to be near him.

Dad had been sick on and off for the last year. I could see the worry behind my mother's eyes when she'd speak of it, but I didn't know the seriousness of the problem. When Dad and I would play checkers, he'd rub his legs, saying they were numb. He didn't have his usual energy, but I never thought much of it, because I was busy with my own life: school, church, and friends.

I zipped up my robe—it was still cold in Omaha in March—and padded downstairs in my fuzzy slippers, unsuspecting of the news to come, thinking I might be told when Dad would walk through the door and into my life again.

As I turned the corner to the kitchen, I saw Buzz Krause, a close friend of my father's, leaning against the counter. Looking haggard, with whisker stubble and dark circles under his eyes, he worked up a sad smile for me. My two older brothers were standing there looking uncomfortable.

The smell of early morning coffee hung in the air. I wondered why we'd been assembled.

After a long pause, Buzz spoke. "I hate to be the one to break the news, but your dad died this morning." Then, after hugging each of us, he said, "I'm sorry."

Looking for some indication that this news was false, I searched for Grandma. Huddled in the corner of the kitchen, she cried quiet tears. My oldest brother, Joel, put his arm around me and squeezed me toward him.

So it is true, I thought, as the news sped through my veins like poison. *Dad is gone, and I didn't say goodbye. This can't be happening. What have I done to deserve this kind of loss?*

The last time I'd seen Dad, he'd been packing. After taking a new job, he had to travel to New York for a meeting. He'd become sick on the plane, which had landed in Chicago in order to get him to a hospital.

I was used to his packing. Dad, a chemist, was often out of town. Sometimes he'd take me with him on summer days when his trips weren't too long. Those times of riding on interstates and highways alone with my dad were what I thought heaven would be like: hours alone with my father, when he had nothing to do but listen to me talk. We'd stop at roadside cafes and eat lunch. I'd feel grown-up and important—Dad always made me feel that way.

As the days after his death blurred by, the thought that I had not had a chance to say goodbye to my dad gnawed at me. Like a plague, it grew, infecting every waking moment, touching everything around me. It hurt, as I slowly realized there would be no more days of flying kites together. No more bedtime chats. I could do nothing to change his death. I knew that. All I wanted was a final goodbye. But a goodbye would never happen; he had already left.

I'd been raised to believe in God. We went to church, and I was taught to pray, to believe. But my prayers had consisted of simple things, things I could imagine God answering, such as passing a math test. I'd never prayed for God to do the impossible. The God that I'd learned about in Sunday school had parted the water and healed the sick. He'd given sight to the blind and fed thousands on a few fish and loaves of bread. But those miracles occurred centuries ago. They'd happened to famous people with great faith. *They couldn't come to pass today*, I decided. *Not to a little someone like me.* Or could they?

Who could I ask? Who would know if God still answered difficult prayers? I felt so alone without my dad. He used to answer the hard questions. With him gone, I decided to ask God directly.

It can't hurt, I reasoned. I needed to talk to someone, and the God I'd been taught about seemed kind. So I prayed, pouring out my sorrow, trusting that God would hear me in the same way that my father used to listen, with patience and understanding.

I wept, storming at God with my 14-year-old passion, looking for understanding into my dad's death. When the fury in my soul quieted, I pleaded, "If you could, please, God, just let me say goodbye."

A week after Dad went to heaven, I had a dream so vivid I smelled the fresh grass and felt the wind tossing my hair. There I stood, on a green mountain, high up—so high, I believed I could touch the clouds. I could see no sun, yet light gleamed all around. Next to me stood my father. With his arms held out, he took my hands.

"I didn't want you to go," I said with urgency in my voice. I was crying. "How can I live without you?"

He smiled his warm smile at me. "I know you'll be fine. I've just come to say goodbye." He looked peaceful and younger than he had during the year before his death.

I nodded, knowing this was the goodbye I'd prayed for. "I love you, Daddy. Goodbye."

"I love you, Emily. Goodbye," he said, letting go of my hands.

I woke with tears on my cheeks, knowing that God had given me what I'd asked for. Now I know, with conviction, that God can still do the impossible.

Emily Allen Hoffman

To Him I Say Farewell

Each one should use whatever gift he has received to serve others, faithfully administering God's grace in its various forms.
—**1 Peter 4:10**

When my principal, Mr. Staples, called me to the office in the middle of the day, I was prepared for the worst. When he told me to have a seat, I could not have guessed what would come next.

I had built a reputation around the school for working well with computers. So when Mr. Staples asked me if I would go to his friend's house and teach him about his computer, it came as no surprise. Then his voice grew serious. He told me to think about my decision, because his friend, Bill, was dying of lung cancer. He assured me that it was completely up to me whether I went or not.

My heart began to beat faster. This was one of those life-changing moments, a test of character. *Could I go to this man's house knowing how sick he was and that he would die soon? No one close to me had died before. How well could I handle it?* I thought to myself.

As all of this raced through my head, I told him I'd do it. He stared at me in bewilderment, and I stared back. Had I really just made the decision so quickly?

I took Bill's address, and on my next free afternoon, I headed over to his house. While driving there, the butterflies in my stomach were dive-bombing my ribs. I had to make another big decision: how would I act once inside the house? I finally decided as I pulled into the driveway that I would be as cheerful as possible and not let my pity show.

As soon as I walked into the house, I knew I was going to be fine. I introduced myself to Bill and his wife, Florence, and he immediately jumped on my last name— Murphy. He asked who my parents were, but I explained to this Kentuckian that we were from Maine, so he probably wouldn't know them.

It turned out that Bill was very involved in genealogy, so that was the first thing we did on the computer. I showed him how to search for genealogy on the Web while he told me stories of his ancestors. He even got out his grandfather's Purple Heart and told me all about how he had earned it in a war. After a while, we spent more time talking than we did on the computer.

In the short time I spent with Bill, I became very close to him. Since all of my grandparents live out of state, he became just like a grandfather to me.

Once, when he was in intensive care after a surgery, I went to visit him. I slipped past the doctors and into his room and was immediately welcomed with "Murphy!", his nickname for me. He introduced me to some of his family, and during my visit they talked of things Bill had told them about me. Here he was, barely holding on, lying there full of morphine, and he was actually bragging on me.

But the next time I went to his house while he was still in recovery, I could tell that he had lost his high spirits. I could see the strain in Florence's eyes confirming that he had no more zeal for life. I tried not to show my own signs of giving up and attempted to encourage him. As I was leaving, she wholeheartedly thanked me for coming and said that she hadn't seen Bill's spirits that high for a long time.

After a while my visits became fewer and farther between. Then the summer came, and between babysitting and family vacations I never found the time to go see Bill. My senior year started, and I no longer made the time to visit him at all. I thought about him often, but I felt I would be unwelcome if I went to visit since it had been so long. I thought he and his family might have forgotten about me.

Time went on, and my conscience began to bother me more and more often until one Sunday afternoon I could not get Bill out of my head. I was on my way to pick up my sister right down the road from his house when it hit me that I had to call him.

Florence answered the phone in a shaky voice. I quickly explained who I was, worried that she wouldn't know me. She assured me that she remembered, and I asked how Bill was doing. Like that first afternoon in his driveway, the butterflies swarmed my stomach as I waited for Florence to break the silence.

She finally said, "Not well. Bill's dying. The doctors only give him a few days to live." I hesitatingly asked if I could come by. She agreed to let me come over for a few minutes.

Trying to prepare myself for the worst, I came to the door. Florence let me in, and I walked over to the hospital bed where Bill was lying. The once strong and lively man was now lying there helpless, weak and dying. As I walked closer, I saw his face. He was asleep, but his face was twisted in pain. I thought it would be a very quick goodbye when I saw his condition.

But as I came to the side of the bed he opened his eyes, and his face lit up as he proclaimed, "Murphy!" I was just a teenage girl who came to help with his computer, but I realized that he had come to love me.

My heart swelled at his warm welcome, and my thoughts wandered to that first day when I sat in this room with a much stronger Bill. He quickly fell back to sleep, and when he woke up again I said my heartfelt goodbye.

A few days later Mr. Staples told me that Bill had passed away. I started crying, but even in the midst of the pain, not once did I regret saying yes to helping Bill. Knowing him for just that short amount of time impacted my life.

I gave Bill something that came naturally to me, not expecting it to make much of a difference. Now I understand that if I just reach out to others and give from my heart, I can make a difference in every life I touch, no matter how small the gesture may seem.

Patricia L. Murphy, 17

My Dream and My Reality

This is what the Lord Almighty says: "Administer true justice; show mercy and compassion to one another."
—**Zechariah 7:9**

Africa was a dream. It was my dream.

In elementary school most kids wrote about wanting to visit Hawaii or some other exotic paradise. I wanted the Congo. I envisioned braving the rugged terrain of the hot deserts of the Sahara on camelback. I wanted to swim with the penguins in Cape Town. I would successfully navigate the wilderness of the continent. The Zulu chief would invite me to dine beneath the brilliant stars by majestic Victoria Falls. I would feed the hungry and battle against the wild animals... someday.

When I entered junior high, the dream had faded into childish folly and became nothing more than a whim. At the time, I was battling for my sanity and well-being. I began to suffer from severe depression.

When I was 14, I began taking antidepressants, and I felt that I was losing the battle. The summer after my freshman year, I was raped and sexually assaulted by a group of guys, some of whom went to my school. At that point, I thought the war had been lost and that I would never recover. I was diagnosed with Post-Traumatic Stress Syndrome and a serious anxiety disorder.

I changed schools in the winter, but I was hardly able to leave the house. I had no friends, no trust, no faith and no hope. I wasn't able to eat or sleep. I suffered from severe anxiety attacks almost daily. The future was dark and overwhelming. It was no way to live, and I wasn't sure I was willing to live if life was like this. It all seemed hopeless.

The next spring I was hospitalized for depression. I spent a week away from the world, evaluating my own world, the one where I had confined and isolated myself. I knew that something had to give and that I had to change before I could expect anything else to be different.

That summer, I heard that a family that I knew was taking a yearlong missionary trip to Malawi, in central Africa. Half joking, I told them that I wanted to go. About a week later they extended an invitation, as long as I could raise my own funds. My mom agreed to let me go as long as the doctors approved and I did well in school.

At that moment, my life completely changed. I suddenly had clarity and a vision. I knew what I wanted, and I told myself it was now or never. It was up to me to make my dreams happen and to change my life. I had a new battle to fight.

I began weaning myself off the medication and slowly learned to be without it. I took my finals early and ended the semester with a 4.2 grade point average, the highest I have ever earned. And I successfully raised $4500 by sending letters to friends and family who donated money to help the cause.

We left the second week of January. The trip was 22 hours long. I could hardly contain my excitement as we finally touched down in Malawi, a country smaller than the state of Pennsylvania. As the plane came to a stop, I gazed upon the vast expanse of green land. The sky was a deep blue, and the hills seemed to roll on forever. Banana trees and corn freely grew about the land.

The airport was nothing more than one short paved runway and a barn. As I stepped onto the platform and was engulfed by the sweltering humidity, I began to wonder about my decision.

There was nothing there but villages full of poverty and disease. I began to realize Africa wasn't a dream or some daring adventure I had dreamt of as a kid. It was a harsh reality that had now become my reality. Malawi is the most densely populated county in Africa and at that time, one in every three people was infected with HIV/AIDS. I knew that Malawi was on the United Nations' Top Ten Most Impoverished Nations list, but I could have never been prepared for what I was about to see.

The streets were merely dirt and decorated by beggars. Most of those begging were emaciated and starving. Some were missing limbs, and others were blind. I saw a woman covered in dirt and rags. She could hardly sit up, she was so frail. She had a small baby who wore nothing but filth and a cloth diaper. The woman just set the baby down on the concrete and it remained there for hours while she sat and begged.

There was a blind man who sat in front of the bookstore and played a flute he had made himself. I gave him some money, but instead of throwing it into the bucket, I wanted to just touch his hands. I guess I just wanted him to know that someone was there. He gave me a toothless smile, and then he hid the money in the loincloth he was wearing. As I walked away, I heard him scream as two police officers wrestled with him over his little jar of coins. The officers won and walked away, but I saw the old man reach down and pat the money that he had saved.

English is the official language in Malawi, so schools are always in need of English teachers. I helped out with the four- to six-year-olds at the Likabula Bible Institute.

Because these children had never seen anyone of lighter skin in close proximity, they screamed and cried every time I walked into the room. I would smile, and they would run. So I began by sitting near the doorway of the one room school. The next time, I moved in and sat on the straw mats that the kids sat on; the kids were still terrified of me. It broke my heart to upset them so much, but the teacher encouraged me to stick with it.

In the class, there was a boy named Gift who was a daring six-year-old. He possessed bravery and courage and was a royal show-off. About the fourth time I went into the class, I was standing over a table with my back to the children. I felt a little poke on my side, and I turned to see Gift. He recoiled in horror and ran away screaming with nervous laughter as if he had just touched something disgusting, like a bug or slime. Once the kids realized that I wasn't poisonous, the crying stopped.

I don't know how much English I actually taught them, but our smiles and laughter became our universal language.

There was an orphanage just a mile or so from our house, down a winding dirt road just outside of town. We drove up to a colonial-style house with rows and rows of baby clothes hung out on lines to dry. We walked into a very clean and welcoming home. All the babies were out on the porch—35 babies lying about. When we stepped out, Ruth, a Zimbabwean woman who had become the head nanny, handed us each a baby to hold.

The Open Arms Infant Home became one of my favorite places to go. Their mission was to take care of these motherless babies until they were two, and then they would send them back to their villages to be raised by extended family. 65% of the babies died at Open Arms; the directors just wished to make them feel comfortable and loved until they passed away.

Lewis was born in December, and his tiny body fit comfortably in the palm of my hand. He was nothing more than a little skeleton. I fell in love with him immediately. He was so docile he hardly cried, but it was apparent he was in a terrible amount of pain. The first time I held him, it frightened me, because he weighed hardly anything, and all I felt was just warmth in my arms. I vowed to myself that from that day on, I would hold him every day.

Lewis' mother had died in childbirth and had left him and his twin sister, Paulina, in their grandmother's care. Milk was so expensive due to the lack of cows in the area that she fed the babies Coca-Cola for the first few months of their lives. Finally, social services brought them to the Home.

I saw Lewis every day, and I watched him grow and develop, little by little. He slept a lot, but every time I came, he would wake up to play. Then he would rest his head against my chest to hear my heartbeat before he would sleep. He was very sick and yet, miraculously, he survived.

Ruth was five weeks old when she arrived. She was one of the most beautiful babies I had ever seen. Her skin was smooth and perfect. Her eyes were brown and big with long eyelashes, and her head was covered in perfect ringlets. The nannies were in love with her. We were all just thrilled because, according to the doctor, she was healthy. But a week later, she began to die. She had dysentery.

I came in on Friday and saw her lying there, wrapped in a bright pink blanket. I picked her up and held her close. She had no control of her body. It would spasm with each bout of bloody diarrhea. The caregivers could not keep up with changing her, so she sat in her own bloody mess. Her skin was translucent, and sores covered her mouth. The whites of her eyes were gray and rolled around in her head. She screamed in agony, and I realized that I couldn't do much except watch her die. I held her to my heart and sang, "Jesus Loves Me"—the only song I could remember. She was expected to die that day, but her spirit was so strong she lasted three more days. I came in and held her all weekend, all day. I watched her pain and pleaded with her to just let go. I promised her that I would never forget her and that I wouldn't let her story die with her. I told her that somehow, I would tell the world.

Dreams can come alive, and sometimes they aren't what we think they will be. Sometimes they are more powerful. Sometimes they are more profound.

Africa was the dream that became my reality. It was a battle waged in a war, and I realize now that no one but God can win this one. I'm willing to go back to Malawi, to work with him to fight for the millions of AIDS orphans. I want to tell the world about Malawi, about its plight—and about Ruth, because I promised.

My experience there helped me overcome my own struggles as I saw people who could do nothing about theirs. Experiencing the conditions that the people of Malawi live with daily has kept my depression from returning, knowing that they so have so much more to overcome every single day.

I am a completely different person now. I have gained an understanding of life, its joys and its hardships. I also understand that there are things that are beyond my control.

Most importantly, I realize now that my dream was bigger than I could imagine.

Vanessa Hernandez, 17

I Begin With Christ and I End With Christ

Neither height nor depth, nor anything else in all creation, will be able to separate us from the love of God that is in Christ Jesus our Lord.
—Romans 8:39

It was the 15th of May. I was having a perfect day with my dad: one of those father-daughter days. He had invited me to his church, so I ran to call my mom to ask her if I could go. She said that I could, but that I might not want to. She hesitated, and then she quietly told me that one of my friends, Chris Sechrist, had died in a car crash the night before. He had been driving down the road when another driver lost control and caused a head-on collision.

To tell you the truth, I didn't believe her. It just seemed impossible to even consider that Chris was gone. Just to see if it was true, I went to my church that morning instead of going with my dad. Sure enough, the whole service was about Chris. All the people were talking about him and crying.

My mom took me to the visitation because I really wanted to go. On the way there, I got really nervous and scared. I knew that it wasn't going to be easy. I took a deep breath, opened the huge door, and walked in. We went to the room where Chris' body was, signed the guest book, and looked at his life album. Then I saw Chris' body in the casket. That is when I finally realized that he was dead.

Everybody was really nice, even people whom I'd never met before. After talking to Chris' dad, I looked for Sherri, Chris' stepmom, who taught me in children's choir when I was growing up. Her usually vibrant face was drained of any color and she looked really lost.

As soon as she saw me, she called out my name and literally fell into my arms crying. It was so hard to hear her anguish coming through the never-ending sobs that filled the room. I knew there was nothing that I could do to help her; I couldn't reverse what had happened and bring Chris back. I felt helpless, too. In my grief, I could think of nothing to say. I just held her for a very long time until her sobs quieted. She let go of me and looked at me with sad, red eyes and barely whispered the words, "I love you." Tears were now streaming down her face. I can't explain how hard it was to get the words, "I love you, too," out of my mouth. My voice cracked in the middle and I sort of croaked them out. We both broke down and cried some more, together.

I looked over her shoulder and noticed that a lot of other people were crying. Chris had meant so much to so many people. It was very hard to say goodbye to him. He had so much more yet to do in this life. Only God knows why he didn't get to stay and see his dreams come true.

That night I tossed and turned in bed, unable to fall asleep. So I began to pray. I prayed through the night, continuing on for about six hours. After that, even though I was exhausted, I felt more at peace about Chris' death. God heard my prayers and sent peace to fill my broken heart with the most comforting thought: *And the peace of God, which transcends all understanding, will guard your hearts and your minds in Christ Jesus.*

Then I recalled how Chris always used to say, "I begin with Christ and I end with Christ:" Christopher Sechrist. For him it wasn't just a saying. I realized that because of his faith, he had never been out of Christ's grasp and that he could never be apart from him, no matter what.

Even through the pain and loss, I learned something: I realize now how truly valuable we are to each other. That night at the visitation, I felt how important I was to Sherri. It felt good to be there for her. It showed me that anyone can help another person in a seemingly helpless situation. It makes no difference how old we are or if we are experienced in such things.

Chris' death also showed me that we don't have to wait to grow up to make a difference. As terrible as it was, his dying really changed my life. He gave me the gift of realizing how important forgiveness is, and what matters most is how we treat each other while we are together.

Tanner Puryear, 13

Tears of Joy

Though he brings grief, he will show compassion, so great is his unfailing love.
—**Lamentations 3:32**

I've got this friend—let's call her "Joy." Joy has a very challenging life: her parents are divorced, and she doesn't like her mom's boyfriend. Joy's mom came on one of our church's youth trips as a chaperone and embarrassed Joy beyond imagination. Joy took care of her mom and refused to comment—showing Christ's love to her mother though her mom was hurting her inside.

One thing about Joy is that she never cries or shows that she's sad. She is always the one to listen, care, cheer you up, laugh, and have fun with you—but she never lets herself be vulnerable enough to cry. Through her strength she shows her weakness.

Sometime in the spring of my freshman year, Joy came and told me that her mom was pregnant, that the father of the baby wasn't nice to her mom, and that she didn't know what to do. A week later she told me that her mother's pregnancy had complications and that her mom had miscarried. Joy never cried. We talked matter-of-factly, and that was the end of it.

Life went on at full speed for both of us in a thousand different directions. Summer rolled around. Life was good—eventful, at least. One day in July my dad called my brothers and me up to Mom and Dad's room. "We're pregnant again! Isn't it great?!" It was great news, but I still fought with myself. *Why now? What will this do to my life?* I selfishly thought. I got angry at life, because it wasn't feasible to be angry with God. It took a month, but I realized my error, and I fell in love with my unborn sibling.

My whole family went to the second ultrasound in October to see the first glimpse of our baby boy that we had named Zechariah David. The nurse was eerily quiet. Then she left the room and talked to the doctor. He told us that Zech had problems and probably wouldn't make it to term.

Shocked silence permeated the ride home. *Oh, Lord, no, not after I love him so,* my heart screamed. *Why us, why this baby?*

Life at home was tense but hopeful. God's will would be done. I waited, knowing reality would slap me across the face, knowing something significant was happening, knowing my own powerless insignificance.

Those two weeks were long: full of school, doctor visits and disbelief. Finally the day arrived, and Mom went to have another ultrasound. When she came home with Dad, I saw her face, and I knew. Time stopped. I was once again reminded of my helplessness. I could not stop my mother's pain, or my family's. My precious Zech had died.

The next day was awful. I walked around school like a zombie. I couldn't cry. I wanted to, but no tears would come. That evening I went to the hospital. Zechariah David was there. He fit in my two hands, swollen, red, and altogether beautiful. I held him, and the tears came. My family cried over him and prayed. I felt so broken, so betrayed.

One of my friends took me to church later that night. The service was over, but everyone was still there. I stumbled in, vision blurry, right into the arms of Todd, my youth pastor. Then there was Joy. She spread her arms, and I saw her eyes. They were full of tears, and as I walked toward her, they began to stream down her face. She simply wrapped me in her arms, tears silently pouring from her hazel eyes. Joy never once let her guard down enough to cry for herself; yet for me, there she was, vulnerable and shameless.

"I know, Aria. I'm so sorry," she whispered, and held me tightly.

We stood there for a long time and just cried together.

The next month was dark for my family as we came to terms with death, all of us in our own battles that none of the rest could fight. Those battles were hard, and the journey was long, but I could never forget Joy's tears, shed so painfully and lovingly.

I remembered them as my mom struggled to cry, to let go, and to continue living without letting death defeat her life.

I remembered them as the next month dragged by, as I was tempted by depression.

I remembered them as I realized that in crying those tears, Joy had finally faced death. God had used Zech to help Joy. God had used Zech for me, too, and he had taught us about himself. He blessed me with Zech, even for such a short time.

The memories are sweet, though it was a dark battle through questions of "why" and "how" and "does God really care." Death is painful, and the natural inclination is to doubt if God truly is love—but Joy's tears showed me otherwise. In her tears and in the tears of others, I saw how God had planned, loved, and shaped each of us—my family, Zech, and Joy—and has given us to each other. He made each of us unique and has plans for each of us.

Aria Guy, 15

07

He is a God of
Love

"...God is love. Whoever lives in love lives in God, and God in him."
—1 John 4:16

"...And I pray that you, being rooted and established in love, may have power...to grasp how wide and long and high and deep is the love of Christ, and to know this love that surpasses knowledge— that you may be filled to the measure of all the fullness of God."
—Ephesians 3:17-19

"For great is his love toward us, and the faithfulness of the Lord endures forever. Praise the Lord."
—Psalms 117:2

By the Grace of God

The grace of our Lord was poured out on me abun-dantly, along with the faith and love that are in Christ Jesus.
—1 Timothy 1:14

It was my freshman year in high school. Drama, cheerleading, and a 3.8 GPA took up the majority of my time, until I met him.

He was in my class. He was an athlete, a singer, and also a Christian—at least, I thought he was. I guess I had the notion that if he were a Christian, our relationship would be somehow immune to the sexual temptations that the average teenage relationship has to deal with. So not true!

We began dating, and during the summer between freshman and sophomore year, our relationship got pret-ty physical. I found myself not knowing how far was too far. We never had a conversation about boundaries, and we were often alone together. My relationship with Christ was put aside, and my priorities were arranged according to my desire to be with my boyfriend. I was seriously neglecting my friends by spending all my free time with him. So I didn't have my friends' advice when I needed it the most. No one was there to confront me and hold me accountable.

After the homecoming dance my sophomore year, we went back to the apartment where I lived with my mom. She was sound asleep. That night we both lost our virginity. I felt a heaviness on my heart and a deep sense of guilt. A few days passed, and I was able to rationalize the guilt. Sex became a regular part of our relationship.

Despite my internal chaos, I managed to maintain an apple-pie facade. My grades were still good, and my parents thought I was an angel.

We were almost caught in the act several times. On one occasion we were completely naked in my living room with all the lights out, and my mother, too embarrassed to be seen in her pajamas, didn't venture out of her room. But she did call out to me from her doorway to make sure that it was me "making all that noise." It's hard to believe she never walked in on us.

After more than a year, the relationship started to go sour. He was drifting away from me and was spending more and more time with his friends getting into trouble. I was using sex to keep him from dumping me. In September of our junior year, he found himself in trouble with the law... and I found myself pregnant.

My morning dilemma was not about figuring out what to wear to school; it became about struggling to keep food down and make it to school. My mom was suspicious, and she decided we needed to take a trip to the doctor. The dreaded moment of truth came when the doctor returned with the pregnancy test results. One of the hardest things I have ever had to do was to look at my mother and try to explain how this happened. I panicked and lied, saying that we had only done it a few times.

She was crushed. My dad was furious when he found out, and my three older sisters were shocked. By the grace of God, all of them turned out to be extremely supportive in the end.

My boyfriend, on the other hand, despite his promises to change and help in the raising of this child, ended up running away from the situation altogether.

My son was born at the end of my junior year, most of which I had missed. I had the summer to learn how to be a mom, and then it was back to school in September for my senior year. I was determined to graduate on time. In order to do so, I had to take six courses both semesters because of the time that I had lost the previous year due to my pregnancy.

There were myriad stressful situations I had to learn to deal with.

I was still nursing when I went back to school, and I remember telling my fourth-period teacher that I might be late on occasion because my breast milk let down right around the time his class started, and I had to change my nursing pads. He was a brand new student teacher and the look on his face was priceless.

I struggled to stay awake long enough to get my homework done late at night after I had put the baby to bed.

I was working every weekend just to pay off my hospital bills.

In order to help out with expenses for the baby, I had to supplement my income by applying for public assistance. Shopping was quite an experience. It felt like everyone in the store was staring at me while the checker stamped and counted each and every food stamp.

The fact that the father of my child was out partying and having sex with other girls added to the stress and trauma of the situation—and it broke my heart.

The dream that I had envisioned of a cuddly little baby being rocked in my arms in the middle of a beautiful nursery filled with everything I needed, including the father of the child, was so far from my reality that it forced me to look outside myself for deliverance. I couldn't do it anymore. I needed more help than any person could give. I needed God. The more I started to realize and accept this truth, the easier things got.

It was so hard to let go of the relationship I had had with my boyfriend. I still found myself wanting to fix it; I wanted it to work out for the sake of our child. I finally had to accept that God knew better, and I was able to let go and focus on the Lord.

That June I graduated on time and with honors. I was ready to move on and start my adulthood. It was then that I began to see how my family's continuous prayers had paid off. I found a new church and a renewed faith in Christ. Most importantly, I was able to recognize that God still loved me and was waiting for me with open arms no matter what I'd done.

With this gift of grace, I began a brand-new chapter in my life. This time, I wasn't going to compromise my relationship with God. This time, God was going to remain right where he belongs—in the center.

Ami Garcia

The Sisters

Then they asked him, "What must we do to do the works God requires?" Jesus answered, "The work of God is this: to believe in the one he has sent."
—John 6:28-29

As a youth pastor, I am frequently greeted by unusual and challenging counseling situations involving wonderful young people who just drop in and dump a pile of hurting inner turmoil on my desk, seeking my help to fix it. They know that I love to see them and that they are always welcome.

One afternoon, two sisters came to me near tears with one of the saddest confessions I'd ever faced—not a drama-filled confession, but one so moving that it made me consider the ways in which I communicated God's love to teenagers.

To help our small-town sheltered youth become aware of the larger world, I had purchased a youth group lending library that we housed in our youth room. Lots of kids took advantage of these stories of people who had done wrong but found hope and deliverance in Jesus Christ: prostitutes who saw the light, thieves who reformed after hearing that God loved them, drug lords, and crooked men and women who changed and followed Jesus.

We had stories of spies who once persecuted the church and how they ended up defending it. Many of the stories became part of our youth meetings as the kids shared what they had learned from the accounts. At church camp we shared the impressions these stories left upon us to hundreds of kids. The challenges of these testimonies had begun to bear fruit in the lives of many: teenagers were talking about entering the ministry or becoming missionaries. The library was a genius decision on my part—or so I thought.

The afternoon that the sisters, both high schoolers, walked into my office was a dreary, rainy one. Usually the girls were bursting with energy and joy. Today they were obviously sad, and the younger one was a bit nervous. Both appeared ready to cry. I immediately wondered if someone had died.

They said that they wanted to talk to me about their lives and relationships with God. The older sister began by saying that she doubted if she was really a Christian. Her sister nodded in agreement. Both were struggling with their faith and needed to know how to become a real Christian.

To say that I was surprised would be an understatement. I asked them what prompted these feelings of uncertainty. I knew for a fact that both girls were dedicated to God and loved Jesus. They were among the first to volunteer for any activity or event that reached out to help others. Now, before me, I could see their doubts and anxiety and could not figure out what had prompted these misgivings.

The sisters asked me to go to our youth room for their explanation. Silently we walked the length of the building, my own apprehensions growing with each step. The girls walked with their heads down, avoiding my eyes. I became increasingly worried.

In the youth room they went straight to the shelves of testimonials by those who were lost but now were found. In a small voice, the older sister told me that these books had shown her that she couldn't be a Christian.

"I have never done anything bad enough or wrong enough to get as much of God's love as these people have received. God saved them from horrible lives, but I haven't done any of the things they have done. Each of these books talks about how God's love was more real to the people in them because they had lived against him for so long. I've just always pretty much worked to be good and to live as God wants us to live. I haven't tried drugs. I don't drink. I am still a virgin, and I want to do the right things. There is just nothing for God to save me from."

I was stunned. My precious library of stories of rogues and thugs was communicating the wrong message to these wonderful kids, and likely to the rest of my youth. They thought one had to be a person of great sin to be loved by God. I knew I had to give this issue some thought.

In the following weeks at our youth group meeting I told the kids how much they pleased God by actively and sincerely living in ways to honor him. In the presence of my prized testimonials I began sharing the blessings of Jesus' words in John 20:29, "Because you have seen me, you have believed: blessed are those who have not seen and yet have believed."

It opened us to such wonderful discussions about living for God that we all became more aware that God lovingly and willingly delivers us from whatever it is in our lives that is contrary to him.

It is far better, we all learned, to live for God without the baggage of some horrendous sin that will take its toll on our lives and memories. It is much better for all of us when we choose God first and avoid the dramatic rebellion that many unfortunately select.

The lesson of these two sisters has directed my work with youth for 20 years. The lost are important to God, but the found are equally precious, and according to Jesus, hold a special blessing all their own.

Rev. Mark A. Simone

One Good Turn Deserves Another

"... For I was hungry and you gave me something to eat, I was thirsty and you gave me something to drink, I was a stranger and you invited me in, I needed clothes and you clothed me, I was sick and you looked after me, I was in prison and you came to visit me."
—**Matthew 25:35-36**

It was a typical Sacramento fall morning: one of those days when the cold, white fog hangs in the air like a wet blanket. I had been working as a pastor at a local church for only about a year, and I was still getting used to the pace of ministry. I was working alone in the church office; too busy to even notice the season's change of colors. That's when he walked in.

He was about six foot two or so, a thin, tall young black man with scraggly hair and a tired, broken-down look on his face. His dirty denim jacket was as tattered as the Army duffel bag that was slung over his shoulder. He looked like a transient. A bum.

When he walked in I immediately and unconsciously put myself on the defensive. *Who is this guy? Is he looking for a handout? Or does he intend to rob me?* But he simply greeted me politely and then asked whether the church had an extra Bible he could have.

Now, I'm not a very good judge of character, but he seemed to be pretty genuine. We started talking.

It turned out that he was living behind one of the nearby supermarkets. For food, he'd been eating the stale doughnuts that the bakery had left out in the back of the store. I gave him a Bible, and then for reasons I don't fully understand, I felt the urge to do something more. So I took out a pen, scrawled out my home phone number, and told him that if he ever needed help, to call me.

As he left, I said two short prayers: first, a prayer for his protection and safety; and second, a prayer to God that he wouldn't actually call. *Please God*, I thought. *Don't let him look me up. You have no idea how busy I am right now.* Since then, I've learned never to pray prayers like that.

That evening I received his phone call. He wondered if he could stay overnight. As I drove over to pick him up, a thousand thoughts ran through my head. *What am I getting myself into? This guy could stab me, rob me, and throw me in the river. And I'm bringing him into my home, with my wife and two toddlers. What am I doing?* But there was something about this situation that I could not ignore. Somehow I felt that this was of God. This was something God wanted me to do. And so I picked him up and brought him home, and we fed him and offered him a long, hot bath and a clean razor.

That night, my wife and I listened to his story and helped him through his tears. Then we prayed with him, and sometime that night this faceless transient became a person to me.

Keith was a professional boxer at the tail end of his career. At one time, he had been rated in the top ten in the WBA standings, but now time was starting to catch up with him. He was the son of devoted Seventh Day Adventists, and his father was once a heavyweight boxer who had been friends with George Foreman and had actually fought Muhammad Ali.

Keith had gotten caught up in some bad relationships with people who were heavily into drugs, and he had a nowhere marriage with three children. Somewhere through all of the incredibly bad luck he had had and the equally incredible bad decisions he had made for himself, he decided to run away from his life. That's why he was living the way he was.

At the time, I didn't know exactly what God's plan was, but I knew he was up to something. I could tell that God was tugging at Keith hard—tugging at him to make major changes in his life. But what I didn't see was how God was changing my perspective, allowing me to see people the way he sees people—with kindness, goodness, mercy and love.

After a week of giving Keith rides, buying him some clothes, and just being someone he could talk to, he began the process of re-establishing his relationship with his parents, getting out of his drug relationships, and even getting a job. We even visited his family and hometown church. It was something to see my children playing with his children at his parents' house. You see, somewhere through all of this, Keith had become my friend.

During the next few years, I lost contact with Keith. Then one day, someone showed me an article in the local paper. It was about a tall, skinny, light-featherweight boxer who had been taking a morning jog. Along the way, he saw smoke pouring out of a house. He ran to the burning home, knocked out a window, and saved the family inside.

It was my friend, Keith.

I've never saved anyone from a burning building. I'm not a hero like Keith is. I was just someone who was willing to be Keith's friend.

Manuel Luz

From the Rubble

Ask and it will be given to you; seek and you will find; knock and the door will be opened to you.
—**Matthew 7:7**

My parents began a major renovation of our home the day before I was diagnosed with childhood leukemia. Obviously they wouldn't have taken on such a disruptive project if they had known what was coming. Before they knew it, they had a house all torn apart and a daughter in the hospital for weeks at a time. I had to have chemotherapy, and it caused all my hair to fall out. That was hard. I would cry often because of all that was happening to me— the shots and surgeries were wearing me down.

During this time, my mom noticed that the center stone of her wedding ring was missing. She was so unhappy, because the ring was very special to her. It seemed that everything special to her was falling apart. She looked all over our messed-up house, in her car, everywhere—but she could not find the diamond.

Months later I contracted the chicken pox while I was on chemotherapy. Normally chicken pox isn't that big of a deal, but when you have it while on chemotherapy, it is life-threatening. Now everyone was even more worried, but we all kept praying that I'd make it through.

One day my grandma was sweeping around the construction in our torn-up house. As she swept, she prayed that God would give her a sign that I would be okay. Before she could finish her prayer, she noticed something sparkling in the six-foot pile of rubble of dirt, wood chips, and lots more. She bent down to see what it was. There in the rubble was my mom's diamond. Right then my grandma knew everything was going to be all right with me. Sure enough, I'm healthy and fine and have been in remission for eight and a half years.

Now every time we look at Mom's wedding ring, it reminds us that God answered our prayers and gave us a sign of hope, assuring us that he cares and that he listens.

Brooke Chandler, 13

I Will Go On

Blessed is the man who perseveres under trial, because when he has stood the test, he will receive the crown of life that God has promised to those who love him.
—**James 1:12**

When I was in the eighth grade, my best friend, John, died of leukemia. I felt so alone. He was the only one who knew the truth about my family. I was sick of the abuse. I was fed up with coming home to a household where my things were sold for crack and weed. I hated having to lie in one place for an hour or two at a time so that the cops wouldn't see anyone in the house and break down the door to arrest them.

John was the only one who cared, who made me feel like I was loved. I had other family, but they had their own problems. They didn't need me as an extra burden. So every morning, after the previous night of abuse, John would sit there and let me dis my family, and when I broke down crying, he would always hug me and reassure me that it would get better.

I believed him for quite some time. I believed that my alcoholic father would stop hitting me and my mom and stop calling me filthy names. I believed that my cousin would stop molesting me.

Then, after nearly three years, suddenly my best friend wasn't there. He had been sick for awhile, but I never really accepted that he might die.

When John died, I sank into a depression. I no longer thought things would be okay. In fact, I didn't know what I was living for anymore, so I planned my suicide. I got close to trying it, but I was really scared, and I didn't want to upset my mom. My mom was the only person alive whom I really loved, even though she wasn't there for me all the time.

For months I agonized over whether to kill myself, run away, or just try to talk to someone about what I was feeling. I remember going from boyfriend to boyfriend looking for affection. I got affection all right, but each relationship ended when I wouldn't have sex. I hated my cousin for what he did to me, and I hated him for making me feel dirty. My bitterness towards him depressed me even more.

Several months later, on the invitation of a friend, I started attending a church a mile or two from my house. I realized that although I had prayed to receive Jesus when I was younger, I had never really known what it meant. In the next few weeks, through conversations with the youth pastor, I learned a lot about Jesus, and when I discovered his great love for me—so great that he gave his life for me—I could hardly believe it.

For the first time, I accepted Jesus with a whole heart. Slowly but surely, my life began to change. I made many commitments and promises to God, promises to stay pure and to do my best to live for him.

It wasn't always easy, but thankfully my youth pastor, Keith, was there to listen to me and help me stay on track. He basically took me into his family and treated me like his own child. He would gripe at me for making a B just like he would any of his own children. He was really the only father I'd ever known. If I had a problem, I went to him. My dad was never there for me that way, so I was really fortunate to have Keith in my life, guiding me and looking out for me. He and his wife, Julie, also never ceased to pray for my family and all the stuff they were going through. They were both just amazing.

Now it's been four years since I accepted Jesus into my life, and nearly everything about me has changed. I am a very happy and upbeat person, and I'm involved in many different clubs and service organizations at school and at church. My friends get annoyed with me because I won't shut up about Jesus. At school I'm known as "Miss PG" because I only watch G and PG movies, and I don't touch drugs or alcohol, because I am doing my very best to keep my heart, mind, and body pure.

I no longer go from guy to guy or question why I should live. I know that I have everything to live for, and I have the only love I need: Jesus. I know I have a very bright future ahead of me, and that's what keeps me smiling. People always wonder why I'm so happy, and more than a few have asked me what I'm high on. I just tell them, "It's Jesus."

I know that I'm not perfect. I have screwed up my testimony more times than I can count, but I am optimistic. I know that I am loved, and I know that I will be okay, because I have the Lord.

Though my family hasn't changed, I am praying for them, and they definitely notice that I'm different. It's hard living there with everything opposing my faith in God and my commitments, but that only makes me grow stronger and more independent each day.

I no longer allow my dad, or anyone else for that matter, to abuse me. The day finally came when I'd had enough, and with my faith that God would keep me strong, I found the courage to call social services. I stood up for myself, and he has finally backed down.

I also no longer have the low self-esteem that I lived with most of my life. In fact, I have confidence in myself, and I know that I am special and that there are people who love me. I have everything I could ever need and want, and I will go on.

Kimberly Marie, 17

Where I Belong

"... But if serving the Lord seems undesirable to you, then choose for yourselves this day whom you will serve...But as for me and my household, we will serve the Lord."
—Joshua 24:15

We were "attached at the hip," as some would say. That was the friendship I shared with Melissa, my childhood best friend. I knew her inside and out, and we told each other everything. We cared about each other, and her non-relationship with God had never been an issue for me. But the closer I grew to Jesus Christ, the more I realized I needed to share my faith with Melissa. I had always attended a Christian camp during the summer, so, thinking that it would be the perfect opportunity to introduce Melissa to God, I invited her to come along with me to camp.

Surprisingly, she agreed to go, which filled my heart with joy. I began praying every night for a life-changing experience for my friend.

In mid-July, Melissa and I headed to camp to spend one solid week with God. I had high hopes of introducing her to a new life. But Melissa was very quiet and kept to herself during that week. She didn't accept Christ; yet I was hoping that deep in her heart a seed for God had been planted. When we returned from camp, she became very distant with me and didn't make any effort to call or contact me.

One evening, I called her and invited her to a Christian concert. She said no, and after we hung up, I began to sob. It was obvious to me that Melissa had rejected God at camp and that she had no desire to be involved in anything related to God. I was beginning to feel that all my prayers for her to have a relationship with Jesus Christ had been wasted. I thought to myself, *God, why are you doing this to me?*

For several weeks, there was no further communication between Melissa and me. Occasionally I would talk to her online, but the conversation was dead. Melissa was not acknowledging me, because she didn't want anything to do with Christians. It was as simple as that.

It was then that reality struck me: that the one thing I had hoped would change her life forever had literally torn us apart. Taking her to my Christian camp had killed our friendship.

Days later the truth was revealed to me in a conversation I had with a mutual friend of ours. It was made clear that my faith, my relationship with God, and my love for him was too much for her to tolerate. Camp had definitely been an eye-opener for her. She could no longer feel comfortable around me.

By now I was convinced that taking Melissa to camp had been a mistake. I worried myself sick over how she could ignore her one and only best friend since childhood. Why would she want to throw away so many memories because of my faith? So many thoughts consumed my mind. I even toyed with telling her that I would forget God just so we could remain friends.

I was a mess. I felt like I had just been shot. I couldn't believe my best friend had betrayed me. I cried so much, my tears were consuming me. Just the mention of her name made my eyes swell with tears.

After many nights of crying, praying, and reading God's word, I began to realize that I never really lost my best friend, because God is my best friend. To him, I am special—maybe not to Melissa, but in God's eyes I am. I know that there must be a purpose for losing my friendship with her. I just have to trust God in that.

I'm still sad about losing a friendship that took most of my lifetime to build, but I'm a stronger person for all I've been through. And I never thought God could heal my heart, but he came through for me by helping me be at peace with myself.

I finally stopped beating myself up for taking Melissa to camp, realizing that I had never even considered the risk of her rejecting God, or me. And in the end, she still heard the Good News. Many people never get the chance to hear it.

Someone once said, "Whether you are happy with your life shouldn't be determined by others' reactions and opinions, but by your own." Melissa didn't like me living for God. But I like living for God and giving him all that I can, because I know that I can trust his faithfulness and love for me.

I am where I belong, and I feel good about that.

Yasmine Shaharazad, 15

Soul Food

I have set you an example that you should do as I have done for you.
—John 13:15

"Thank you, ma'am," he said, accepting the bologna sandwich I was offering.

"You're welcome." I looked into his eyes, red-rimmed and rheumy. Even at arm's length I could smell his body odor—the result of weeks, or maybe months, of not washing. "God bless you," I said.

The words disappeared in the warm summer air as fast as the man vanished into the crowd of those who'd already received their sandwiches and were queuing back up for seconds.

Another man, cleaner than the first, took his place. As I handed this one a sandwich, the mild Santa Ana wind blew dust from the dirty parking lot all over my new Bass loafers. I frowned and took stock of my grungy surroundings—the corner of Fifth and Wall in the heart of Los Angeles's skid row—the place where the "down-and-outers" of society lived. These were the people who slept in refrigerator boxes—the ones who protected themselves with the kind of knives the man shuffling in front of me was wearing shoved into his belt.

I sucked in my breath at the sight of the weapon, and the question that had been playing in the back of my mind came bubbling to the surface. *What's a nice Jewish girl like you doing in a place like this?*

I had been raised in a Jewish home. My mother lit the Shabbat candles every Friday night, ushering in the Sabbath. At Passover, my two sisters and I helped her remove all the food products in the house that contained yeast, readying the cabinets for the unleavened Passover food. At Chanukah we spun the dreidel and ate latkes—crispy potato pancakes—piled high with sweet applesauce. Mom taught us the importance of charity, one of the tenets of Judaism, and we gave some of our allowances to the poor.

But though our family was Jewish, we did not live in a vacuum. We saw Christian movies like *The Robe* and *Ben Hur* and watched children's TV shows with a Christian message.

My best friend, Rita, was a gentile—pure Irish Catholic. We went everywhere together; I even walked with her to church on Saturday mornings. When Rita stepped into the little black booth to make her confession, I waited, sitting in the church pew, looking up at the face of Jesus.

There was something about Jesus' face that I liked. But I had been taught that he was the gentile's God. Jewish though he was, Jews did not believe he was the Messiah.

Around the age of 14, I began to grow restless in my faith. To me, Judaism was more social than spiritual, and I felt no personal connection to God. A hunger for that connection began to form in my heart.

So I searched for God in various disciplines of the New Age movement, studying meditation, yoga, past life regression and reincarnation, but nothing satisfied the emptiness inside me.

In the early '80s my search was temporarily diverted, as the plight of the homeless began making headlines. Each time I saw a program about the hapless state of these street people, I was driven to tears.

One day, after months of crying, I asked myself, *Bev, what are you doing to help?*

The drive to do something was so strong I contacted a pastor acquaintance who worked with the homeless. He encouraged me to join a food ministry he knew about which made and distributed sandwiches to the poor. *I could do that*, I thought.

But just as quickly another thought came. "They're not all born-again Christians, are they?" I asked. I had negative notions about Christians—especially the "born again" types. I didn't want any uptight Jesus Freaks buttonholing me, shoving a Bible in my face. I was a Jew. I wasn't interested in trading in my pastrami-on-rye for a ham-on-white! It was one thing to investigate other religions, but quite another to convert, turning your back on Judaism and your people.

Still, that Saturday night found me at the house of a Christian in the San Fernando Valley. He ushered me back to where loaves of bread sat atop long tables and showed me how to make the standard-issue sandwiches.

One by one, other people arrived and took their places beside me. I had expected little old church ladies and pompous men in suits and ties, but most of them were kids just past their teens. *It's Saturday night*, I thought. *Why aren't these young people out partying?*

But although it was ministry, it was like a party—everyone laughing, smiling, joking around.

These were average, everyday kids, and yet there was something different about them. They seemed to genuinely care for one another—and for me, a stranger.

Week after week I made sandwiches, never having the nerve to venture into the streets to give them to the homeless. Nobody tried to convert me. But each week as we met to slap together the meat and bread, I had questions.

They encouraged me to study both the Old and New Testaments—especially books like Isaiah and the Psalms that foretold of the coming Jewish Messiah.

Everything I read seemed to point to Jesus. But while Jesus claimed that he was God, Jews believed he was only a great teacher. That seemed to make more sense to me. After all, how could God be a man?

I remained unconvinced until the day the kids talked me into riding down in the van with them to the street to pass out the sandwiches we'd made the night before.

Skid Row was worse than I had expected. In an empty parking lot in the seediest part of town, I saw 150 people, mostly men with tattered clothes and filthy hair, lined up, waiting to be fed.

A man with rotten teeth came close and talked to me. I felt my stomach heave at the smell of his breath. Before I had a chance to escape back to the van, Robert, one of the leaders of our group, thrust a large paper bag overflowing with sandwiches into my arms. "Hand these out, will you, Bev?" Seeing the stricken look on my face, he laughed, adding, "...and tell them God loves them!"

"Okay," was all I could say.

When all the sandwiches were gone, the ministry broke into small groups of twos and threes, gently approaching the homeless men and women standing and eating. I stood back and watched.

"Is there something you'd like prayer for today?" I heard Shelly, one of our group members, ask a bedraggled mother holding tightly to her lean little boy. The woman nodded.

Shelly reached out and took the woman's rough hands in her own. The moment she did, the woman burst into tears. Shelly moved closer and cradled the woman in her arms. Then she closed her eyes, and together they prayed.

For an hour I watched as this scene was repeated— this comforting of men and women who were dirty and smelly, possibly even riddled with lice. Big men, some of them with weapons, openly wept on the shoulders of these caring Christians.

Suddenly the movie *Ben Hur* and the Bible account it depicted swam into my mind. I remembered how Jesus touched and healed the lepers, the outcasts of society, despite their cries of "Unclean! Unclean!"

There on that hot Los Angeles street, these new friends of mine were being Jesus to the lepers of their day. And suddenly, I knew who God was. He was flesh and blood before me, living out his purpose in those who called him Lord. Their hands were his hands. Their arms were his arms.

Another mild gust of Santa Ana wind hit my face. I looked down at my dusty loafers. *What's a nice Jewish girl like you doing in a place like this?* I asked myself again. Now I had my answer.

I could deny him no longer. My heart reached out for him and a warmth spread through me like an embrace. There I was, one Jew, held in the spiritual arms of another.

I walked forward to a man who was standing alone, his back toward me. I hesitated, then touched the frayed yellow vest that covered his paper-thin shirt. He turned, and as I looked up into his face I saw the heartache in his eyes. "Would you like some prayer?" I asked, touching his shoulder. His leathery skin reflected the sun. It was a good face, a beautiful face.

It was the face of God.

Beverly Spooner

Afterword

"It is God himself, in his mercy, that has given us this wonderful work, and so we never give up. We do not try to trick people into believing—we are not interested in fooling anyone...We stand in the presence of God as we speak and so we tell the truth, as all who know us will agree."
—**2 Corinthians 4:1-2 The Living Bible**

"We stand true to the Lord whether others honor us or despise us, whether they criticize us or commend us."
—**2 Corinthians 6:8 The Living Bible**

Got a
Great
God Story?

We'd like to consider it for publication in

TRUE Volume II.

E-mail your story or story lead to:
true@lifewriters.com

Or send it snail mail to this address:
TRUE Volume II
P.O. Box 10879
Costa Mesa, CA 92627

For writing guidelines and more information about
TRUE and TRUE Volume II, log on to
www.lifewriters.com.

If you'd like to read and help us select the stories to be
included in TRUE Volume II, e-mail us at
true@lifewriters.com.

Giving Back

We have chosen to make a difference in the lives of teens beyond those who have an opportunity to read this book. We will donate a portion of the proceeds from the sale of this book to two nonprofit organizations on behalf of the celebrity authors. Both organizations focus on teens and provide them opportunities to go places where there are people in need whom they can serve in myriad ways.

The Center for Student Missions

If Christians are to make an impact for the Kingdom in the 21st century, they must live out the call to be Jesus' hands and feet to the poor and needy. CSM gives young people and adults the opportunity to do just that in North America's inner cities, providing students with an effective urban ministry experience that transforms lives, supports local churches, and honors Christ. CSM currently offers mission trips to:

Chicago, Houston, Los Angeles, Nashville, Philadelphia, San Francisco, Seattle, Toronto, and Washington D.C.

The Center For Student Missions
PO Box 900
Dana Point CA 92629
Tel: (949) 248-8200
csm@csm.org
www.csm.org

Teen Mania

Teen Mania Ministries is committed to sparking a revolution in global youth culture by inspiring a generation of young leaders to develop a bedrock of Christ-like character, a vibrant relationship with God, and a commitment to reach the world with the love of Christ. Their mission is to initiate, facilitate and sustain a massive movement of young people from all over the world for strategic short and long-term missions endeavors by enlightening, motivating, providing opportunity, and plugging them in for life. Teen Mania Global Expeditions offers missions trips to various destinations on the following continents: Africa, Asia, Europe, Latin America, North America and Oceania. For more information contact:

Teen Mania Ministries

P.O. Box 2000
Garden Valley, TX 75771
Tel: (800) 299-TEEN
Fax: (903) 324-8100

Email @teenmania.org
www.Teenmania.com

Irene Dunlap

Irene Dunlap, co-author of *Chicken Soup for the Kid's Soul™*, *Chicken Soup for the Preteen Soul™*, and *Chicken Soup for the Soul™ Christmas Treasury for Kids*, began her writing career in elementary school when she discovered her love for creating poetry, a passion she believes she inherited from her paternal grandmother. She expressed her love for words through writing fictional short stories and lyrics, as a participant in speech competitions, and eventually as a vocalist.

During her college years, Irene traveled around the world on the Semester at Sea program aboard a ship that served as a classroom and home base for over 500 college students. After earning a bachelor of arts degree in communications, she became media director of Irvine Meadows Amphitheatre in Irvine, California. She went on to co-own an advertising and public relations agency that specialized in entertainment and health care clients.

When Irene asked God to direct her to difference-making work that would leverage the talents and gifts she had both acquired and been blessed with, he answered. She soon began working on *Chicken Soup for the Soul™* books, which she believes was all preparation for creating this book to honor God and reveal his true character to teens.

Irene continues to support her two teens with their interests in music, theatre and sports activities. She also carries on a successful singing career, performing various styles ranging from jazz to contemporary Christian in clubs, at church and at special events.

Irene lives in Newport Beach, Calif., with her husband, Kent, daughter, Marleigh, son, Weston, and Australian shepherd, Gracie. In her spare time, Irene enjoys entertaining, traveling, horseback riding, painting, gardening and cooking. If you are wondering how she does it all, she will refer you to her life verse for her answer:

Now glory be to God who by his mighty power at work within us is able to do far more than we would ever dare to ask or even dream of—infinitely beyond our highest prayers, desires, thoughts or hopes.
—**Ephesians 3:20**; Living Bible Translation

If you would like to contact Irene, write to her at:

Irene Dunlap
P.O. Box 10879
Costa Mesa, CA 92627
e-mail: **irene@lifewriters.com**

Permissions and Biographies

Gangster for God.

Reprinted by permission of Alejos Dream-Bear. ©2001 Alejos Dream-Bear.

And we know that all things work together for good to those who love God, to those who are called according to his purpose.
—Romans 8:28

If this scripture were not true, I would not be here today. Thank you, Jesus! You're in control, not I. Roger Dream-Bear can be e-mailed at mail@lifewriters.com.

Huge Twist of Fate.

Reprinted by permission of Audio Adrenaline. ©2001 Audio Adrenaline.

With a music career that spans more than 10 years, Audio Adrenaline has achieved a longevity that only a handful of artists experience in today's fast-paced, ever-changing music industry. With a total of seven studio albums to its credit, Audio Adrenaline is approaching sales of more than three million units and has garnered four Grammy Award nominations and multiple Dove Awards. While the band's focus has always touched on themes of missions and outreach, Audio Adrenaline has never been more aggressive in communicating that message than now, with the release of the album *Worldwide* and participation in developing The Go Foundation in support of youth pursuing missions. Visit Audio Adrenaline's Web site at www.audioa.com.

Under Control.

Reprinted by permission of Josh Auer. ©2001 Josh Auer.

According to Josh Auer, bass player and co-founder of PAX217, some bands turn to music as an escape, a refuge from the pressures and torments of the real world. Others——including the vast majority of what passes for hard rock on mainstream radio and MTV these days—use it as a platform for airing frustration, a soapbox for venting anger. But PAX217 has made it personal. While their music has been dubbed "music for the masses," to the band, it means more than just a popularity contest. Just as apparent as the driving blend of reggae, rock and hip-hop in their music is the sincerity of reaching the audience that they came from. The five young men of PAX217 offer a fresh perspective. And it hits not like a hail of grievances, but rather as a positive instrument for change, for hope.

Filled.

Reprinted by permission of JR Barbee. ©2002 JR Barbee.

JR Barbee lives in Southern California with his wife Danielle. He has been in youth ministry for ten years, and is currently at Living Stone Chrisitan Fellowship in Mission Hills. He and his wife are part of Nitro Praise, and JR was front man of the Prodigal Sons. He can be reached at 13691 Gavina Ave., #439, Sylmar, CA 91342, or by e-mail at jrbarbee@hotmail.com.

It's Your Call.

Reprinted by permission of Dirk Been. ©2002 Dirk Been.

Dirk Been is a youth pastor and speaker who is currently starting 5th Ashton Entertainment, Inc., a film, television and publishing production company. Dirk can be contacted at www.christianspeakers.com.

Who I Am Today.

Reprinted by permission of Mandy Biggs and Karen M. Biggs. ©2001 Mandy Biggs.

Mandy Biggs is a junior in high school and is thankful to be playing softball again after being diagnosed with cancer. Her biggest goal is to show people how much God loves them and that he will always be there.

From the Door of Death.

Reprinted by permission of Katherine Blake. ©2001

You can e-mail Katherine at mail@lifewriters.com.

Set Apart.

Reprinted by permission of Meredith Breitling.
©2001 Meredith Breitling.

Meredith Breitling is an 18-year-old from Texas who values her friends and loving family. She is a member of the Fightin' Texas Aggie Class of 2007.

The Phone Call.

Reprinted by permission of Jennifer Briner. ©2002 Jennifer Briner.

Jennifer Briner is a full-time mom, speaker, and trainer. With an enthusiasm for God that is contagious, she conveys his truth through teaching, music, drama, and dance; she has utilized her gifts to plant churches overseas. Jennifer works at the Baptist Student Union at the University of Missouri part-time on small groups, discipleship, and leadership development with over 200 college students. She lives with her husband, Eric, and four kids: James, Nathan, Rachel, and Emma. You can e-mail Jennifer at jennifer@mizzoubsu.org

From the Rubble.

Reprinted by permission of Brooke Chandler and Doreen Chandler. ©2002 Brooke Chandler.

I'm Here.

Reprinted by permission of Samantha C. Cojuangco. ©1999 Samantha C. Cojuangco.

Samantha Cojuangco is a 20-year-old who is working toward a biology and teaching degree at the College of Mount Saint Vincent in the Bronx, New York. Her biggest passion is singing, and her ultimate goal is to become the voice of a Disney character. She's involved in a million and one different clubs at school and loves working with people. Samantha looks forward to marrying one day and having a family. If you would like to contact Samantha, you can e-mail her at abu2u2@aol.com.

Sudden Death.

Reprinted by permission of Wendy Dunham. ©2001 Wendy Dunham.

Wendy Dunham is a wife, mother, inspirational writer, and registered therapist for differently-abled children. You can reach her at 3148 Lake Road, Brockport, NY 14420, (585) 637-0535, or by e-mail at wendyann@rochester.rr.com.

The Family Across the Way.

Reprinted by permission of Rusty Fischer ©2001 Rusty Fischer.

Rusty Fischer is the author of over 25 published books. He has also written hundreds of articles, appearing in such nationally recognized periodicals as *Better Homes & Gardens, Woman's Day, and Seventeen*. His work has been anthologized in such best-sellers as *Chicken Soup for the Preteen Soul* (HCI) and *Stories for a Teen Heart* (Multnomah Press). Rusty lives with his wife, Martha, in sunny Orlando, Fla.

That Infamous Summer.

Reprinted by permission of Kristen Funk. ©2002 Kristen Funk.

Kristen Funk, 21, is a junior in college pursuing a B.S.W. in social work and a bachelor's degree in Bible. She hopes someday to head up her own social service agency working with children from abused and neglected backgrounds. She enjoys running, hiking, biking, kayaking, canoeing, playing the piano, and writing.

By the Grace of God.

Reprinted by permission of Ami P. Garcia. ©2001 Ami P. Garcia.

Ami Garcia is a stay-at-home mom living in Southern California with her husband and two children. She is actively involved with her husband's youth and missions ministries at Cornerstone Christian Fellowship. Using her testimony, she speaks to youth about making godly decisions about sex and offers guidance to teenage mothers. Contact Ami at 17575 Euclid St., Fountain Valley, CA 92708, or by phone at (714) 962-5412. E-mail her at amiga-7@msn.com.

Grateful in Michigan.

Reprinted by permission of Elizabeth Glover. ©2001 Elizabeth Glover.

Elizabeth Glover graduated in 2002 from West Catholic High School, where she wrote for the school newspaper and won three statewide writing competitions. She is studying communications at Michigan State University and is involved with the Haiti Program, a "twinning parish" program involving missions, cultural exchanges and financial support to the villagers of Seguin, Haiti. She can be e-mailed at gloverel@msu.edu.

Tears of Joy.

Reprinted by permission of Aria Guy, Cindi Guy and Ty Guy. ©2001 Aria Guy.

Aria Guy, 16, loves learning about God, dancing, laughing, reading literature, writing, and stargazing. She feels blessed to have three brothers and parents who love God and each other. She thanks her family for teaching her to love the good, the true, and the beautiful.

How Sweet the Sound.

Reprinted by permission of Cynthia M. Hamond. ©1999 Cynthia M. Hamond.

Cynthia M. Hamond, S.F.O., began writing five years ago. She has been published in several *Chicken Soup for the Soul™* and *Stories for the Heart* books and magazines and has received two awards. Her story, "Goodwill," published in *Chicken Soup for the Kid's Soul,™* was made into a TV movie. You can reach Cynthia at candbh@aol.com.

Traveling on the Same Track.

Reprinted by permission of Patricia Hathaway Breed. ©2001 Patricia Hathaway Breed.

Patricia Hathaway Breed lives on the rugged coast of Northern California. She spends her weekends teaching painting and ceramic sculpture to students with disabilities at the College of the Redwoods. She and her husband enjoy watching the sun set with their granddaughter and German shepherd on the ocean bluffs. Contact Patricia via e-mail at breed@mcn.org.

My Dream, My Reality.

Reprinted by permission of Vanessa Hernandez. ©2001 Vanessa Hernandez.

Vanessa Hernandez lives in Southern California with her dog, Beau, and attends Orange Coast College as a sophomore. She is working to create a teen crisis counseling office called G.U.T.S. (Girls United Together for Strength) to help teens who have been sexually assaulted. She encourages anyone who has been sexually assaulted to tell someone. She can be e-mailed at vhernandez_guts@msn.com.

My Secret Life.

Reprinted by permission of Daniel J. Hill. ©Daniel J. Hill.

If there's one thing that should be known about Danny, it's that he's a Christian. Compared to following Jesus, everything else is secondary to him. The one thing he wants to get across is this: "Jesus' grace is sufficient to heal all hurts and forgive all sins. That's why I love him."

Let Me Say Goodbye.

Reprinted by permission of Emily Allen Hoffman. ©1998 Emily Allen Hoffman.

Emily Allen Hoffman is a news writer, feature writer, and columnist for the newspaper *The Wauneta Breeze*. She also writes books for children and magazine articles for a variety of different publications. In her spare time she likes to lift weights and make jewelry. She lives in Nebraska with her family. She can be reached at emily@emilyallenhoffman.com. Visit her Web site at www.emilyallenhoffman.com.

Perfect Waves.

Reprinted by permission of Bryan Jennings. ©2002 Bryan Jennings.

Changes.

Reprinted by permission of Bryan Jennings. ©2002 Bryan Jennings.

Bryan Jennings is a professional surfer who started the Walking on Water Foundation, a Christian nonprofit organization dedicated to sharing the gospel of Jesus Christ. Since its inception in 1995, the organization has grown nationally and internationally through outreach events. Bryan can be reached at Walking on Water Foundation, PMB 624, 3830 Valley Centre Dr., Suite. 705, San Diego, CA 92130, via e-mail at info@walkingonwater.org, or at his Web site at www.walkingonwater.org.

Tire Tracks.

Reprinted by permission of Jason Kennedy. ©2001 Jason Kennedy.

The band Cadet is based on the philosophy of always striving to be more like Christ. Cadet, formed in 1999 from the remains of two Oregon-based bands, signed with BEC Recordings in the fall of 2000 and has recorded three albums: *Cadet Self-Titled* (2001), *Any Given Day: Earth to Heaven* (2001), and *The Observatory* (2002). For more information about Cadet visit www.cadetland.com.

The Age of Silence.

Reprinted by permission of Leah C. Koop ©2001 Leah C. Koop.

Leah C. Koop, 24, appreciates the fact that she has had the opportunity of a second chance. Her adoption experience still has an effect on her life. Leah has spoken to high school students, sharing with them her experience and perspective on adoption. Because Crisis Pregnancy Center and Bethany Adoption Services played such a big role in supporting her adoption, she promotes these organizations to others. Leah is working on her degree at Vanguard University and holds a full-time job as a pharmacy technician. She is engaged to be married to an awesome Christian, Brett, whom she met at V.U.

Overnight.

Reprinted by permission of Renee Krapf. ©2001 Renee Krapf.

Renee Krapf loves to keep a journal and write short essays and poems. Ministering with the Center for Student

Missions for more than six years has given her many real-life faith experiences to share.

Building Blocks.

Reprinted by permission of Phillip LaRue. ©2002 Phillip LaRue.

Phillip LaRue, 21, is an accomplished musician who has produced three CDs with Reunion Records. The band LaRue recently released an album, *Reaching*, to challenge the culture to understand who God is. Throughout Phillip's life and career he has had a passion for others to see the character of God. His desire for the future is to be real and vulnerable, no matter which door God leads him through.

Accountability.

Reprinted by permission of Nikki Leonti. ©2001 Nikki Leonti.

Nikki Leonti has two records out in the Christian music market and is currently working on a new project. She tours regularly performing her original music and also speaks to young girls about abstinence through Crisis Pregnancy Centers and Mercy ministries. Nikki currently resides in Nashville, Tenn., with her daughter Jaslyn.

One Good Turn Deserves Another.

Reprinted by permission of Manuel A. Luz. ©2001

A worship pastor by calling and an artist at heart, Manuel Luz is also a songwriter and musician with dozens of album credits and independent releases. Of his previous life as an aerospace engineer he says, "It doesn't take a rocket scientist to go into ministry." Manuel lives with his beautiful wife and four children in Vancouver, British Columbia, and currently serves as a worship pastor for South Delta Baptist Church. His Web site is www.manuel-luz.com.

I Will Go On.

Reprinted by permission of Kimberly Marie. ©2001 Kimberly Marie.

Kimberly Marie, 19, was born and raised in Dallas, Texas, was recently married and plans to begin her certification to become a Christian children's counselor. She enjoys singing, reading, cross-stitching and children. Her favorite verse is Philippians 4:13—"I can do all things through Christ who gives me strength." Contact Kimberly at kimbers15@yahoo.com or visit her Web site at www.geocities.com/kimmytheprincess/.

From Fear to Hope.

Reprinted by permission of Deb Matthews. ©1999 Deb Matthews.

Although born in Texas, Deb Matthews counts herself a native of Washington State. She is a motivational speaker and teaches leadership courses for Boeing as well as the adult Sunday School at her church. Her hobbies include reading, writing, hiking, and working with youth in puppetry. You can e-mail her at deb@debauthor.com. Visit her Web site at www.debauthor.com.

To Him I Say Farewell.

Reprinted by permission of Patricia Murphy. ©2001 Patricia Murphy.

Patricia L. Murphy is a 22-year-old graduate of St. Louis University where she earned a bachelor's degree in aviation and earned a professional pilot's license. She has spent the past year in Ecuador as a missionary for Rostro de Cristo where she taught English to middle school students, helped in an after-school care program, and taught computer skills to adults at a technical school. Patricia's fluency in Spanish enabled her to participate in the local church choir while in Ecuador. In the future, Patricia hopes to return to South America and utilize her piloting skills to assist mission organizations.

Owning Up.

Reprinted by permission of Joe Nixon. ©2001 Joe Nixon

Joe Nixon has drummed for the five-member SoCal punk band Slick Shoes since its inception. The band has recorded its fifth full-length album, *Far From Nowhere*, on the Los Angeles-based SIDEONEDUMMY Records with legendary rock producer Ed Stasium. It's hard to believe that, not too long ago, the band unexpectedly landed its first record contract with Tooth & Nail. At the time, lead singer Ryan Kepke was a mere 14 years old and had only been a member of Slick Shoes—his first and only band— for two weeks. Nixon prefers to describe his band's manic music as simply "fast, fun, and melodic...I guess it's punk, but that word is used so loosely nowadays."
Slick Shoes joined the 2003 Warped Tour and at press time, planned to continue gigging around the world for at least eight months out of the coming year.

Out of the Muck.

Reprinted by permission of Brian Pikalow. ©2002 Brian Pikalow.

Rev. Brian Pikalow, known as Pastor Pik, is Family Pastor at Asbury United Methodist Church in Maitland, Fla. He led the Fellowship of Christian Athletes (FCA) in high school and at the University of Central Florida. After graduating from college, he worked as an electrical engineer for the Navy until returning to the FCA in 1994. He was later called to the student ministry at Pine Castle United Methodist Church, and the student ministry grew from 33 to over 300 students in two years. He assisted Pat Morley with his new book *Young Man in the Mirror*, a companion work to *Man in the Mirror*, which sold over a million copies. Pastor Pik can be contacted at pastorpik1@cs.com, (407) 644-5222, or at www.40days.net. He encourages his readers to hear his father's side of the story. Contact Dennis Pikalow to speak for your church or organization at (610) 696-5884 or by e-mail at swiftee14@cs.com.

I Begin With Christ and I End With Christ.

Reprinted by permission of Tanner Puryear and Dana Marsh. ©2000 Tanner Puryear.

Tanner Puryear is a sophomore in high school who enjoys playing piano, singing, and acting. She loves writing, especially poetry, and her mom is her inspiration, best friend, and biggest fan. Her number one passion in life is God, and she is active in her church.

Miracle on Mother's Day.

Reprinted by permission of Aaron Redfield. ©2001 Aaron Redfield.

Paid in Full.

Reprinted by permission of Aaron Redfield. ©2001 Aaron Redfield.

Aaron Redfield recently became a pastor after completing an internship at Horizon Park Chapel in San Diego, California. A drummer by trade, Aaron has recorded and toured with enough bands to have lost count—some of the noteworthy ones are Switchfoot, Jennifer Knapp, Out of Eden, Charlie Peacock and Rebecca St. James. For two years, he did studio work in Los Angeles, recording for movie scores such as *Orange County*, *The Good Girl*, and an upcoming sequel to the VeggieTales movies. He is currently playing with the Dance Floor Prophets, a kind of alternative acoustic band that travels around to prisons as well as college towns. The band sets up on street corners and ministers to passersby, playing for free and developing relationships that will hopefully lead non-believers to Christ.

Really Real.

Reprinted by permission of Stacey Robbins. ©2001 Stacey Robbins.

Stacey Robbins does music with her husband, Rocky, and travels around the country with her message of encouragement through music and speaking. With her stories and songs, she hopes to comfort others with the comfort she's received. She has a son, Caleb, who is showing signs of being a drummer already. You can reach Stacey at 427 E. 17th St., Box 123, Costa Mesa, CA 92627, by phone at (949) 863-7655, or by e-mail at common-ground@integrity.com. Her Web site is www.common-groundministries.com.

Michael's Gift.

Reprinted by permission of Chelsea Rollert and Amanda Rollert. © Chelsea Rollert.

Chelsea Rollert is the oldest of four children. She has a sister named Brooke and two brothers, Michael and Gabriel. She plays basketball and softball and is a cheerleader. She is also on a club volleyball team and enjoys spending time with family and friends.

Speaking Up.

Reprinted by permission of Lauren A. Schara and Larry Schara. ©2002 Lauren A. Schara.

Lauren Schara, 17, lives with her parents in Indiana. She would like to attend the American University in Cairo, Egypt, next fall. She aspires to become a United States ambassador to Egypt. She enjoys going to Christian rock concerts with her friends.

Where I Belong.

Reprinted by permission of Yasmine Shaharazad. ©2001 Yasmine Shaharazad.

Yasmine Shaharazad enjoys playing the guitar, and everything she does involves music. She also enjoys going to church, attending concerts, and spending time with family and friends.

Desires of the Heart.

Reprinted by permission of Tracy Simmons. ©2002 Tracy Simmons.

Tracy Simmons grew up with a pen in her hand and a ball at her feet. She has a passion for three things: God, soccer, and writing. She recently graduated from Eastern New Mexico University and feels this book is a stepping-stone in her life. You can e-mail Tracy at simmonswriter@yahoo.com

The Sisters.

Reprinted by permission of Mark A. Simone. ©2002 Mark A. Simone.

Rev. Mark Simone has been in youth ministry for over 24 years. He has spoken and trained throughout the U.S., Eastern Europe, and South Africa. Mark has written many articles and four books on youth ministry issues. He lives in Chagrin Falls, OH, with his wife, four kids, and a grandson. Contact Mark at 76 Bell St., Box 60, Chagrin Falls, OH 44022 or via e-mail at msimone@fedchurch.org. His Web site is www.fed-church.org.

My Mountaintop Experience.

Reprinted by permission of Emily Smith and Melinda Elgin Smith. ©2001 Emily Smith.

Emily, a senior in high school, plans to attend American University in the fall. Emily is active in the Federated Church as a Sunday School teacher, a confirmation teacher, and a youth group participant. She loves the outdoors, reading, writing, drama, and especially her family. Emily tries to bring her faith into each of the hobbies in her life. Thanks to her church family, Emily has expanded her faith into every aspect of her life as a guiding force in all she does. She would like to thank her parents, siblings, friends, and, of course, God for the endless support.

Soul Food.

Reprinted by permission of Beverly Spooner. ©2002 Beverly Spooner.

Beverly Spooner has been a member of The Society of Children's Book Writers and Illustrators for the past seven years. Her recent children's story, "Just Desserts," appears in *Chicken Soup for the Preteen Soul*. Her works consist of feature articles, stories, and poetry. In the 1980s she was a contributing reporter/writer for *The Topanga Messenger*. Beverly lives in Naperville, Illinois with her artist husband, Michael, an artist/art director for Disney and other animation studios. Bev gets some of her inspiration for children's stories from their son, Philip, and their two lovable mutts, Rembrandt and Snowy. Bev can be reached at http://www.scbwi-illinois.org/Spooner.html.

The Door's Open.

Reprinted by permission of Sid Stankovits. ©2001 Sid Stankovits.

Sid Stankovits was born and raised in California. He married Jennifer Smith on October 7, 1996, and together they have one son, Jonny. Sid owns a tattoo parlor in Santa Ana, California where he specializes in Christian tattooing. He's currently organizing the first-ever Christian tattoo convention. For more info, log on to www.rockofagestattoofestival.com. If you'd like to check out his designs and more about his work, go to www.sidstattooparlor.com.

In God I Trust.

Reprinted by permission of Andrea Stephens. ©1996 Andrea Stephens.

When she's not playing ball with her golden retrievers, working on an oil painting, or munching on a piece of pepperoni pizza with extra cheese, Andrea Stephens is usually writing a book for teen girls or answering questions in her column, "La Glamour," in BRIO magazine (Focus on the Family's publication for teen girls). She lives in Bakersfield, California, with her handsome pastor. Oh, he's also her husband! She can be reached at P.O. Box 2856, Bakersfield, CA 93303, or by e-mail at andrea@andreastephens.com, or via her Web site at www.andreastephens.com.

Solid Rock.

Reprinted by permission of April L. Stier. ©2001 April L. Stier.

April Stier is currently a senior at Bethel College in Mishawaka, Indiana, with a double major in English/writing and Biblical literature. April has a wide range of writing experience. She served as copy editor for Bethel's yearbook during the 2000-01 school year and has been a contributing writer for the yearbook and campus newspaper for four years. She has published articles in *Encounter*, *Guideposts for Teens*, and *Emphasis on Faith* and Living. April also reviews books for Church Libraries and is currently editing dissertations for two of her professors, one of which will be published by Cambridge University Press. April uses her free time to go on adventures with her friends and volunteer as a youth sponsor in her local church's senior high youth group.

The Bottom Line.

Reprinted by permission of T-Bone. ©2001 T-Bone.

With a musical resume that stretches over a 12-year period, Flicker Records/Boneyard Records recording artist T-Bone is credited with bringing the true West Coast street sound to the Christian hip-hop arena. T-Bone's contribution to the industry has not been merely his longevity but also his relevance to the genre and the cultural influence it has on this generation. His career began in 1991 with the JC Crew, and T-Bone followed with a string of innovative solo projects that included *Redeemed Hoodlum*, *Tha Life of a Hoodlum*, *Tha Hoodlum's Testimony* and the compilation *Tha History of a Hoodlum*. He hasn't veered from that stylistic path on his newest release, *Gospelalphamegafunkyboogiediscomusic*, another musical milestone for an artist who remains focused on delivering an uncompromising message with a fresh, authentic hip-hop twist.

On the Other Side.

Reprinted by permission of Haley Vile. ©2002 Haley Vile.

Haley Vile developed a passion for writing while traveling and is amazed at the impact her writing has on others. She is attending college in San Diego, California, to become a teacher. She can be reached via e-mail at seaweed61@hotmail.com.

The Only True Peacemaker.

Reprinted by permission of Adrianne Webster. ©2001 Adrianne Webster.

Adrianne Webster is a senior at Texas A&M University. She has two adorable Chihuahuas, Sage and Kelbi. She plans to return to A&M to get her MBA degree. She can be contacted at sage11@cox-internet.com.

Truth-filled.
Timely.
Encouraging.

More favorites from **invert**

0-310-24971-6

0-310-25559-7

0-310-25408-6

Available at your local Christian bookstore